Valentino The Unforgotten

T RACY R YAN T ERHUNE

Bloomington, IN Milton Keynes, UK

authorHOUSE®

AuthorHouse™
1663 Liberty Drive, Suite 200
Bloomington, IN 47403
www.authorhouse.com
Phone: 1-800-839-8640

AuthorHouse™ UK Ltd.
500 Avebury Boulevard
Central Milton Keynes, MK9 2BE
www.authorhouse.co.uk
Phone: 08001974150

First published by AuthorHouse 4/11/2007

ISBN: 978-1-4259-9673-4 (sc)

Library of Congress Control Number: 2007901560

Printed in the United States of America
Bloomington, Indiana

This book is printed on acid-free paper.

FOREWORD

My book *Valentino Forever* paid due homage to the unique Hollywood tradition of the memorial services held annually for Rudolph Valentino at Hollywood Forever Cemetery.

Without a doubt - Valentino *is* forever.

Since then, I have received letters and e-mail from London, Germany, Italy, Japan, as well as all over the United States. They thanked me for writing this untold part of the Valentino legacy. Several of them closed their letters by inquiring as to what my next Valentino project would be. At the time I didn't think there would be another project. *Valentino Forever* was supposed to be a one-shot deal.

I originally planned to re-publish *Valentino The Unforgotten* as a supplemental addition at the back of *Valentino Forever*. However, when *Valentino Forever* grew to 240 pages, I dropped the idea. To publish it separately was suggested by Virginia Back. After thinking it over, it made perfect sense to re-publish the original book in its entirety that was the inspirational cornerstone of *Valentino Forever*.

Valentino The Unforgotten was released in early 1938 by the Wetzel Publishing Company in Los Angeles California. The sad reality is that only one shipment of books was dispatched from the warehouse before a raging fire swiftly swept through and destroyed not only the structure, but all the books within. Sadly, no copies of Peterson's book escaped the ravish of flames. It was never republished. Only those few copies sent out on that first shipment survived and made their way into collector's hands.

While doing research for *Valentino Forever* I enlisted the Library of Congress to do a copyright search/verification on *Valentino The Unforgotten*. After they reviewed the official records, they certified that Peterson had never renewed the copyright and thus the book was officially now in public domain.

While I quoted several stories from Roger Peterson's book in *Valentino Forever*, I felt that his book should be made available once again. Complete and unedited, exactly as Roger C. Peterson wrote it.

That is what you now hold in your hands. Now everyone can enjoy as much as I have - the truly fascinating, insightful and colorful story that Roger C. Peterson witnessed day to day at the crypt of Rudolph Valentino.

Tracy Ryan Terhune

This edition of

Valentino The Unforgotten

is respectfully dedicated to its author

Roger C. Peterson

ACKNOWLEDGEMENTS

No project of this type could ever be completed without the kind assistance of people who shared my goal to see this story told, or in this case re-told. I am deeply grateful to the following people for their ongoing generosity help and encouragement.

I am indebted to Marc Wanamaker for providing gorgeous photographs of the cemetery buildings and grounds. Marc's company Bison Archives retains a wealth of rare photographs pertaining to early Hollywood history. Thanks to Marc Wanamaker we can turn back the pages of time and see Hollywood Memorial Park Cemetery as it looked when Roger C. Peterson worked here.

Michael Back and Virginia Back are two treasured friends who generously assisted this project by providing access to several of their vintage photographs. They have been at the helm of acquiring rare Valentino photos and material for decades. Their collection is legendary. The idea of re-publishing this book was first suggested to me by Virginia Back.

Jim Craig gave me the opportunity to acquire the complete files and correspondence of Ditra Flame when I had started writing *Valentino Forever* in 2001. Those very same materials proved to be of great assistance on this project as well. Jim also assisted in my search for where Roger Peterson was buried.

Stella Grace was the first person I met when I attended my first Valentino Memorial Service in 1996. She has become a close friend, as well as supporting this project. Stella and I collaborated on the creation of a permanent exhibit for Rudolph Valentino at the Hollywood Heritage museum, using items from our own personal collections.

Donna Hill is another close friend. Donna created the first comprehensive Valentino website online, and today it remains unequalled. She has helped me many times over and I am most appreciative of her ongoing support for all my various Valentino projects. She has done much in her own right to honor Valentino's legacy, and its always been done with class.

Many thanks for various help, suggestions and support of this book: Tammie Kadin, Jeff Masino, Emily Leider, Marvin Page, Michael Yakaitis, Hollywood Heritage Museum, the staff of Grand View Memorial Park Cemetery, downtown branch of the Los Angeles Public Library, Samantha Tibbs of Hollywood Forever Cemetery, the helpful staff of the Los Angeles County of Records, the Norwalk, California division. Rock Armstrong, Max Hoffmann.

Thanks and appreciation to Hollywood Forever Cemetery, Tyler Cassity, Jay Boileau, as well as my friends Irina Sokolova and Anna A. Ovsepian from the Hollywood Forever Flower and Gift shop. You make it happen every August 23rd!

And last but not least, Bosco.

A NOTE ABOUT THIS EDITION

In order to maintain the integrity and flavor of the 1937 publication of *Valentino The Unforgotten,* this new edition is being produced as a mirror copy of the original. Every capitalization, wordage, punctuation, paragraph and sentence structure was reproduced identical to the original. Only a few minor spelling errors were corrected.

CONTENTS

Unforgotten
Vintage Photographs
of
Hollywood Memorial Park Cemetery

Ariel view of Hollywood Memorial Park Cemetery in 1926, the year Valentino was buried there

Front entrance to Hollywood Memorial Park Cemetery, circa 1934

View of the belfry with the bells barely visible at the entrance circa 1934

Front entrance to Hollywood Memorial Park Cemetery, off Santa Monica Blvd, circa 1934

Another view of the front entrance to Hollywood Memorial Park
Cemetery, off Santa Monica Blvd, circa 1934

View of the Chapel at Hollywood Memorial Park Cemetery, circa 1934

Interior view of the Chapel, circa 1934. It was here on August 23, 1927
that the very first Valentino Memorial Service was held

View of the lake as well as surrounding grounds, circa 1934

Another picturesque view of the lake and surrounding grounds, circa 1934

This view gives a glimpse of the ornate William Andrews Clark Jr. mausoleum
which the lake surrounds. Clark was the founder of the Los Angeles Philharmonic,
and died in 1934. Photos from 1923 show the structure fully completed

Ariel view of Hollywood Memorial Park Cemetery circa 1923

Exterior front view of the Cathedral Mausoleum, circa 1934

Impressive view of the main entrance corridor to the Cathedral Mausoleum, circa 1934. The bottom portion of the stained glass was removed in 1951 to extend the mausoleum for the proposed Court of the Apostles. When those plans were abandoned, the eight foot carved marble statues of the Apostles were lined up in the main corridor, where they remain to this day. It is right here in this corridor that the Valentino Memorial Service has been held for decades every August 23rd

Roger C. Peterson, right, and an unidentified assistant place a
floral tribute at Rudolph Valentino's crypt, circa 1938

DEDICATION
TO
THE SPIRIT OF
RUDOLPH VALENTINO

PREFACE

To those who seek a full biography covering the life of Rudolph Valentino, the books "Valentino As I Knew Him," by S. George Ullman, "Rudolph Valentino; His Romantic Life and Death," by Ben-Allah and Valentino's own diary may be recommended.

There have been magazine articles without number covering parts of Rudy's life, written by different persons who knew him intimately at different periods. An interesting biography was written by Adela Rogers St. Johns and published in serial form in "Liberty" during the latter part of 1929. It revealed many incidents of Valentino's life that have not been contained in other books and articles, many little human touches and revelations. It also, unlike innumerable sensational newspaper and magazine articles, possessed the merit of being true and not found on rumors.

In the April, 1932 issue of "New Movie Magazine" appeared an article entitled "My strange Experiences at Valentino's Grave." It contained much of the author's diary up to that date. As custodian of the resting place of Valentino in the mausoleum of Hollywood Cemetery, my diary has dealt with little else than the experiences encountered there.

The publication of this article brought to me a flood of correspondence from people all over the world, asking a thousand and one questions and seeking further information regarding what I have seen and heard.

In response to these requests, I have undertaken to tell something of what has occurred at the resting place of Rudy. For the benefit of those who are not familiar with his life, I have sketched some of its main facts, in the chapter on biography. The only feature I have added, which is not contained in any of the other biographies, so far as I know, is the analysis of Valentino from the points of view of graphology, numberology and astrology. This addition has been made because of the interest of innumerable admirers of Valentino in these subjects.

The germ of my desire to write this book took life and grew from my amazement at the never ceasing parade of people seeking the Valentino crypt, when there are so few, comparatively, looking for the tombs of others who achieved greater and more sustained fame during their lives.

Valentino's illness, death and funeral were events of international interest. It was not surprising that, following the interment in Hollywood, visitors and mourners were very frequent. But it is reason for surprise that now, eleven years after the man's death, the number of these has increased rather than diminished. It is cause for wonder when numberless persons say to me that the spirit of Valentino has drawn them here. The vast majority of these are deeply and humbly sincere. Allowing for a small percentage of the exhibitionist and neurotic types, they are sane, normal folks, who come here as to a shrine. Their devotion cannot be taken lightly nor regarded as insignificant.

The longer I serve as sentinel of the dead, I become more and more mystified. It is my hope that the following pages will arouse the interest and understanding of others.

It may be well, perhaps, to reveal what sort of person I am. After all, observation is modified by the character and personality of the observer. Born in Duluth at the head of Lake Superior in the year 1903, I am about the age of Valentino at the time of his death. There, the similarity between my subject and myself stops.

Duluth has a wonderful natural harbor. It is the gateway to the beautiful Arrowhead country, the name given to the point of land which extends along the north shore of Lake Superior to Canada. This region is a huntsman's paradise. Here, countless happy days of my youth were spent, in hunting through the forests or fishing in the numberless lakes and streams. Travel was mainly by boat or canoe. A trip of any length meant numerous portages between the lakes.

Later, drawn by a quenchless love of adventure, I worked on a boat plying between Duluth and Port Arthur, Canada. But the West was always calling, and I finally took Horace Greeley's advice. I have worked in tire factories and assembly plants, in sawmills and paper mills, and with railroad construction gangs. I spent a couple of months in the Dakota harvest fields. When I came to California, I secured my present position at Hollywood cemetery.

In this sketch, I have tried to show that I am too normal and healthy a person to be unduly influenced by the uncanny or the mystic. I have not colored my story of the strange and sometimes weird incidents which I relate here. But through these experiences at Valentino's tomb, I have come to ----- "Think of him still as the same. I say: He is not dead. He is just away."

CHAPTER I

"Valentino."

"Rudolph Valentino."

"Will you direct me to Valentino's tomb?"

"Where is Rudy's crypt?"

"I have some flowers for Rudolph. May I – would it be all right if I placed them there myself?"

"Will they let me sit here close to –him—for a little while?"

Valentino, Valentino, Valentino! All day. Every Day. From early morning until the purple shadows lengthen across the marble floor of the massive Cathedral Mausoleum, pilgrims throng to the mecca of their quest, the tomb of Rudolph Valentino. People from all walks of life, all nations, all creeds come to pay homage. Something Valentino has created brings them here. Is it love? Is it hero worship? Or is it the man?

Today was an average day, with some fifty or more visitors. They inquired concerning Valentino, or brought flowers, or asked for a souvenir – a blossom from a bouquet, a petal to press in a book, a bead from a decorative piece….And it is eleven years since Rudy died.

A woman in tears.

A decrepit old Italian with deep wrinkles that write a story of suffering and privation across his face, gnarled hands that tell of a lifetime of toil. Tears in the old man's eyes, a gentle, sad smile. He kneels and crosses himself devoutly. "God bless him! God grant him rest and peace."

An ancient mourner mutters a benediction, limps away with bowed head, his twisted walking stick stabbing at the marble floor.

A young girl in hysterics. She becomes calm at last and departs, sobbing quietly.

A middle-aged woman kneeling in prayer for twenty minutes. She kisses the front of the crypt and walks slowly away with bowed head, shoulders bent, hands folded.

An entire family, father, mother, two sons in their 'teens, and two older daughters, all standing solemn and reverent after placing a great wreath at the tomb. "We came from New York just for this." No other words. A few minutes of silence, and they are gone.

Nine out of every ten visitors to the mausoleum stop at Valentino's crypt. Those who are familiar with its location find their way to the spot unattended. Many of these come back repeatedly. Some appear regularly on the same day of the month or week and at the same hour. Most are solemn and reverent. Some give way to tears each time. Many come once and are never seen again. Many appear in good spirits and unburdened with sadness. Their visits seem to be in the nature of a rite. They come to pay their respects, to bestow flowers. Others merely stand in silence, or kneel in prayer, then depart quickly.

There is neither exaggeration nor a striving for effect in what I give here. I am setting down facts as I know them, in order that the problem which puzzles me may be made clear to others. There must be a reason for these things. I cannot believe that things "just happen."

There is something deeper and more vital in this interest in Rudolph Valentino, eleven years after his death, than the mere memory of his short and brilliant career. Thousands who are drawn to his tomb are moved by more than the memory of his shadow on the screens of the world. If not, why is he singled out for adulation—almost worship—while greater actors and greater men are forgotten? Why is his resting place visited every day of the year by this continuous procession of men and women from near and far? Why do they stand with moist eyes and bowed heads before his crypt? Why do they break into sobs? Why do they kneel in prayer? Why do I receive letters from every corner of the earth from people who want descriptions of the tomb? Why the constant floral offerings?

There must be some cause deeper than idle curiosity or mere hero worship. The fame of this Italian boy, who sprang from obscurity and who died at the age of thirty-one, seems to increase in death as much as it did in the most glamorous period of his life. In that fact lies the mystery.

CHAPTER II

What of all those other illustrious, famous, or interesting men and women who now abide in these acres of eternity in the midst of which stands the mausoleum? Why am I not besieged with questions as to the location of the remains of Thomas H. Ince? Ince was known the world around as director and producer of motion pictures long before Valentino first set foot upon American soil. His name was a household word for many more years than were included in Valentino's entire span of success. He created, made famous, and publicized dozens of stars. His name was emblazoned upon cinema screens wherever motion pictures were shown. His productions were distributed to every remote corner of civilization as well as among the great cities of the world. The peoples of every continent knew the name of Ince.

The news of his death was flashed over the world, extras poured from the presses and were snatched from shouting newsboys by millions of stunned readers. It was a world tragedy.

Yet, not over four or five times a year does anyone ask me where Thomas Ince lies. Meanwhile thousands and tens of thousands who never saw Rudolph Valentino in the flesh come to bow their heads and bend their knees before his tomb.

Barbara La Marr rests in the mausoleum where so many other screen celebrities lie. Christened Reatha Watson, this amazingly beautiful girl achieved success and mounted to heights that carried her through a much longer period of fame than Valentino enjoyed. Barbara La Marr, like Valentino, started as a dancer and died after winning international adulation as a screen star. She was called the "too beautiful girl" by a Los Angeles judge who advised the then Reatha Watson's mother to take her away from the city to the comparative safety of some small town. Literally acres of newspaper space were devoted to this girl's pictures and news of her every move in life. Her succession of husbands kept her sensationally in the public eyes, in addition to her screen triumphs. Her name was known to millions in other countries who would have found it difficult to name the President of the United States.

But, I am seldom asked to show visitors where Barbara La Marr's ashes repose. And yesterday, as I write this, over six score of men and women asked to be conducted to the tomb of Valentino!

William Desmond Taylor, renowned motion picture director, was murdered in Hollywood a decade ago. The murderer was never apprehended and the whole affair remains under a cloud of mystery. William Taylor slumbers here in Hollywood Cemetery while his murder is still discussed, even after all these years. But few come to his resting place. It is rare to receive an inquiry about him.

What screen star was more popular or more widely known in life than Wallace Reid? He was a public idol for years. His "fan mail" came to him daily in baskets. Weekly and monthly publications devoted to news of screen people were filled with pictures of "Wally." Pages were crammed with descriptions of his fads and fancies, his habits, his achievements as an actor, his ability as a musician, writer, artist and amateur chemist. He occupied a place in the hearts of millions of admirers through many more years than were numbered in Valentino's career.

Yet thousands pass his grave in another not far distant cemetery unheedingly.

The list of those who lived in the radiance of fame and whose earthly remains are peaceful in this little city of the dead, is long. Gene Stratton Porter, whose novels were and still are among the biggest sellers. Robert Edeson, veteran actor of stage and screen. Theodore Roberts, beloved of theatergoers of three generations and whose fame extended from stage days of the past through a long succession of triumphs on the silver screen. Frank Keenan, another stage and screen veteran. William Henry Rothwell, leader of symphony orchestras and internationally known musician and composer. William H. Crane, creator of the part of David Harum on the stage and known as one of America's greatest actors for decades. Virginia Rappe, the girl with whose murder Roscoe Arbuckle was charged and for which he was twice tried and finally acquitted. Allan Holubar, Louis Wolheim, June Mathis, the great-hearted girl who wrote so many feature stories for screen production. It was June Mathis who adapted "The Four Horseman of the Apocalypse" for the screen. It was she who practically "discovered" Rudolph Valentino and it was at her urgent suggestion that he was given the part in this production that lifted him to fame almost over night.

That great actor, Rudolph Schildkraut, lies here in the stillness of the mausoleum. A more finished actor than Rudy ever was, yet more than half forgotten in the short time since his death. Jean Havez, writer of songs that have been whistled and sung by millions. Robert McKim. Tom Forman, beloved director who was responsible for a long list of admirable screen productions. Karl Dane is also here, laid away in a grave donated by friends. Karl Dane was an unusual character and fit wonderfully well his parts in silent pictures. But the talkies rang the death knell for him. His accent was a thing he could not change, and he walked the streets from studio to studio, hoping to get a break. His money finally gone, and poor Karl finished it all with a bullet.

These and many others sleep within the marble walls of the mausoleum, or under the tall pines and cypress trees in the surrounding cemetery. Few, if any ask about them.

But Valentino attracts a long line of mourners nearly every day. In death, this man is more loved, more honored, better known and understood than he was in life. Possibly some explanation may be found in the diary which he kept during his first trip back to Europe after he had made a place for himself in America.

CHAPTER III

Valentino's diary, with an introduction by Michael A. Romano, was published in 1929. The following are only excerpts, but they suggest something of the philosophy and characteristics of the man.

June

My dream is coming true!

That is, one of my dreams… I have so many …

And so this will be, in a measure, the rambling record of a dream. A dream come true. From day to day, from night to night, here and there, I am going to write down my impressions. I am going to put down on paper the things I think, the things I do, the people I meet, all the sensations, pleasurable and profitable, that are mine from the moment I pack my first trunk to leave America's friendly shore, until the moment I unpack it again, when I shall have returned once more.

It is a good thing, I think privately to myself, to have a dream come true. For dreams are scarce these days, and realizations even scarcer. They say that only poets and fools dare dream…that is why I attempt to write poetry…!

I am going aboard.

I am going "back home." Home to the old country. Home to my people. And this means more to me than it would to a great many people. It isn't merely a casual return to the old town to say, "How are you? How have you all been?" No it is much more than this to me…

Ten years ago I came to America poor, friendless, unknown and penniless. I didn't know what was to become of me. No one met me when I landed at the pier. No one even knew I was coming, and if they had known, it wouldn't have made the least difference in the world to a living soul. They would have thought, if they had thought at all, "Oh, another poor Italian boy coming to America!" Nothing could be more uninteresting. Another young Italian, coming to the shores of Liberty to make his fortune… if he could. But I wanted more than mere fortune. My ambitions vaulted high above earth and fastened themselves to the immemorial stars. I wanted Fame. I wanted LOVE. I wanted my name to ring around the world. And I wanted that name to awaken love in the world as it went its ringing round.

I shall never go home, I said to myself, until I can go home SOMEBODY.

The mere thought, the poor, thin, fruitless hope of such a thing thrilled me to the very core. To have left, as I left, poor, and unknown, a Nobody. To go back… rich, famous, successful…what a desire! What a dream!

July

Tomorrow we sail.

Everything is arranged. We were only ten minutes in the passport office. The man who took my photograph said, "This is a great pleasure, Mr. Valentino. I hope I prove to be a

5

satisfactory cameraman." I have looked better in pictures than I looked in that one, but it was satisfactory enough for me.

I haven't done any shopping. I decided to get most of my clothes in London, which has also been a long-deferred dream of mine. And besides, I don't mind admitting it in a private diary, the clothes are cheaper there! Even a movie star must grapple with that fact! Natacha, of course, has Paris in mind when she thinks of clothes!

I pack and unpack my last valise. The only new things I have bought are new cameras, so that I may make a picture record of our trip. Natacha tells me that I really should use a small Brownie No. 1, instead of the expensive Graflexes and other intricate cameras I have treated myself to. She says that I always take two or three pictures on the same film. I am a Futurist when it comes to camera work, she tells me. But I am happy doing it. I think I take very excellent photographs. But I shouldn't care to be my own cameraman.

The Next Day

Well, we are on our way!

The ship moves with the slow and stately motion of some magnificent animal plowing a majestic course through the Eternities!

I feel almost impatient with it, as though I should get out, get behind it, begin to push it faster… faster…. Excitement still runs in my veins like a fever…

I did not sleep for more than an hour or two the night before. I would drop off to sleep, then wake up with a start thinking, "Tomorrow we sail! Tomorrow I am going home!" and then I would drop off again for a few moments only to wake up again with the same stirring thought. Natacha slept as little as I did. We lay awake and whispered excited, fragmentary things for most of the night.

At the dock I found a great crowd of people, waiting to see us off. We walked through the crowd with difficulty, but it was a difficulty I loved, because it was the most real and beautiful part of the dream I have put on. Ten years ago on that same dock, I wended a solitary, lonely, slightly frightened and quite friendless way. No one cared. This time with my wife by my side and my wife's aunt, Mrs. Werner, on my other side, I passed between a throng of friends, some whom I had never seen before, but all of whom had seen me, and were there because they loved me and wanted to wish me well.

I love all countries, and all peoples as I want all countries and all peoples to love me. But it is in America that my Golden Opportunity came to me. It is America who gave me the world.

The Next Day

I woke early this morning… our first day out. I could see the waves, curling with a sort of gentleness around my porthole and bending down to meet them, gently curving, too, the dawning sky… I had an impression of the white and tinted arms of beautiful women circling the world. Lying very quietly, so as not to awaken Natacha, I mentally wrote a poem to the impressions that were being borne in upon me by the trackless world we were traveling through… All of my recent difficulties and entanglements, personal and professional, seemed very far away in that morning hour. They didn't seem to matter just then. I knew, vaguely, that they would come back again, that the pressing questions of what I was to do and when I was to do it would bear in upon me, claiming attention, soon again, but for the moment I was held in the delicious arms of poetry and peace.

Sometimes I think that the only thing the Public does not understand about an artist of any sort is his, or her need of rest. The People seem to think we are indefatigable; that we need never be alone, never draw into ourselves to store up new energy, to give them if we can, new delights.

The moon was gorgeous, riding high in the heavens. The water seemed as black as night. I told Natacha that when I had been coming over that first time, ten years ago, the immensity of the whole thing made me feel shriveled up and small and frightened, but that now, with her beside me, with the fruitful experiences of the past ten years as a sort of background of courage, I felt larger than Time and Space. We decided that one must feel larger than Time and Space in order to get along. There are so many things to beat in the world… so many fields of battle to triumph over… We stood toward the back of the ship… Now and then we made some fragmentary slight remark, for the rest, we were silent… it is one of the most perfect charms of life to me to talk to a woman like that… I mean… without effort, detachedly… voicing the random thoughts as they come to me … wrapped and drowned in beauty…

Natacha has said that I am like a child, and I suppose I am. Isn't every artist? For if we did not quiver and react to all of the new and strange sallies of life, of people, of the things that happen to us, how could we, in turn, convey them to the Public? I think that an artist should be the most plastic thing under the sun, responsive to every touch, a sort of victim, as it were, to every impression.

We reached London at midnight in a pouring rain. I had expected to arrive very quietly, with no one but my secretary to meet me. It had been announced that we were arriving sometime that day, but not precisely when, and it never occurred to me that anyone would hang around waiting… To my positive astonishment we found that we were assailed by at least a thousand boys and girls, who had stood all night in the dismal pouring rain, waiting for our arrival.

It was the most spontaneous and thrilling greeting I believe that I ever had… perhaps because it was so unexpected. And at first they were all very courteous and gentle, until I had nearly walked my way out of the throng and then those who had not succeeded in acquiring the desired autograph, began to grow excited and fearful and a sort of hum rose up around us, like a hive in excited action… I did all of them that I could. It was so sweet of them to wait for me like that. I knew that they would have, severally and individually, a difficult time getting to their various homes, as the bus-systems stop work at midnight in London. They

7

had waited a long and dreary time to see me, and the least that I could do for them was to put my name on their pathetic little slips of paper: It was a slight repayal of what they had so patiently done.

We finally managed to locate our car and drove to the Carlton Hotel. The Carlton is under the same management as the Ritz, both in London, here and in New York…

My secretary told us that we had *the* suite, "the" very much emphasized, at the hotel and that the notable set of rooms and the imposing bed had been slept in by a long line of imposing personages before us. Natacha said that we were paying for history, and I said that one could pay for nothing more substantial.

I shall have probably only two or three hours sleep at the most if I keep on writing any longer. Natacha has fallen asleep and I have the sensation of being alone in London… rain falling… a London peopled by the ghosts of all the famous personages of Dickens and history… and friends… friends of mine… waving little white flags of a beautiful truce to welcome me.

In the morning the London Press will be awaiting me, I am told… and in the afternoon I shall go forth to make what I can of London… mine…..

What will it give to *me*?

London, First Day

I have lived my first day in London. And it has in no wise disappointed me. I am always conscious of a certain thrill when a dream lives up to the expectation. Not so very many do.

One dreams of a thing, a place, an event, for a long, long while, and then, just before the dream is to come true, one feels a certain fear. Or *I* do at any rate. Perhaps, after all, the dream won't be all we had thought it, hoped it. Perhaps we are in for a disappointment, a disillusionment. That is how I felt about London. That city of my dreams… peopled with figures steeped in history and the lore of Dickens and Shakespeare… if it should disappoint me…

But it didn't. The London I saw was the London of my dreams. The London of history, and of the great men who have immortalized it with words.

I finally decided that we wouldn't do any deliberate "sightseeing" this first afternoon. I don't know, as I muse over it, that I entirely believe in sightseeing, anyway. It seems to me that just to wander about a certain part of a country, soaking in the atmosphere, absorbing the color, the memories, half consciously, half subconsciously getting the *feel* of the place under your skin, into your blood and veins is a far better way of knowing a city or a country, than going about studiously striving to assimilate facts, dates, names.

I felt, today, as we walked here and there, at random, at will, that London was *my* London, in a sense. That I was speaking to her in my own way and she was speaking to me. We understood one another, London and I.

I believe I am a little peculiar in this respect, in that I do regard pictures with awe and

8

reverence. I feel the screen is a great art, the marvelous possibilities of which have only been vaguely realized, and I will confess that it is my great ambition to make pictures that will constitute great screen art.

I always like to talk to children on their own plane. If I have nothing to say that I think will mean something to them, I try to keep silence out of respect for them, not to talk down to them with silly mouthings that make them despise you, secretly, if not openly, in the prideful depths of their dignified little souls.

I love children. And I would like, some day, to have a large family of them. People speak of romance... well, but the heart of romance lies, a lovely, tremendous bud, in the heart of a child – in the hearts of all the children of the world. Children *are* romance. They are the beginning and they are the end. They are romance, before the white wings are clipped, before ever they have trailed in the dry dust of disillusion.

I felt that "vague, sweet melancholy" that pervades one when one says good-bye to a very old friend, when I left London. We were becoming old friends, London and I. A bond had been established. Some time in the very long, long ago, English blood had stirred, by happenstance, in my veins. Sometime in the long ago one of my ancestors had trod English soil, only to be merged again into Italy. But none the less, I felt what the students of heredity would call the "throw back" moving in my veins. We knew one another of old London and I.

France

When we alighted at Le Bourget, there must have been four hundred people there to meet us.

In one sense I was more touched than I was even at the reception accorded me in London. For, after all, in London my films were fairly well-known. They were more in touch with what I had been doing, with what the film world in general is doing, in America. But in France I had anticipated no such recognition.

I think it was that reception that gave me, or emphasized, at any rate, the feeling I new have of warm love for all the countries in the world. Thus far on my trip I have been made to feel, so pleasantly, that much talked of state of beatitude, the Brotherhood of Man. All peoples are my friends, and what more tremendous thing could happen to a man than this?

We all know how precious friendship is. We all, or most of us know how *rare* it is, when it is real. When it is true. We have heard, and thought, that if a man has one friend upon whom he can rely, or, at best, two or three, he is indeed blessed among men.

Hebertot, hand outstretched, first greeted me. And then I shook hands with as many as could reach me before we were whirled away in Hebertot's car to the Hotel Plaza-Athenee, the best Hotel in Paris.

On the ride over, Herbertot told me that a great dinner had been planned for us the same night, at which would be the most of the editors, actors, authors and other celebrities in or about Paris at that time. He told me that they are intensely interested in the cinema of America, and how we work, and all about studio conditions and production activities and the like.

I told him that I was never so happy as when discussing with interested and intelligent persons, the questions nearest to my heart, and that I would be only too happy to answer their questions, I hope so intelligently as they would be put to me.

And this is indeed the truth. I am never so happy in conversation with others as when I am discussing the future of the screen – the opportunity that exists to make it one of the great arts in the world today. It's a sort of passion with me. I love to discuss it and I don't believe any task could be too big – any amount of time too great, for me to undertake or devote in making pictures better than in many instances we find them today.

Still farther along the same line, both in Paris and London I was not only questioned intelligently and interestedly, but I was also *quoted correctly*. No single one of them took "poetic license" or any license at all with what I told them. It was an enormous satisfaction and one for which I am immensely grateful.

There is virtue in a weed quite as much as in an orchid. And there is beauty in a weed, too, if it is growing, rank and sweet in its own surroundings and not trying to insert itself into some priceless Cloisonne, where an orchid should be placed. If you have the Cloisonne, well and good. Then if you will dwell in it gracefully and rightfully, fulfilling your destiny in the place appointed for you. But if you were born by the country roadside and circumstances have not environed you differently, why break your heart about it, with the result that you are neither the sweet–smelling garden weed, nor yet the aristocratic orchid?

Sometimes, when I have spent an evening in such a place as the Casino here at Deauville, when I have seen the spent and wearied and tragedy-smitten faces of the men; the hardened, painted, pitifully striving faces of the women, I think how much better it really is to be the humble blades of grass that know the pulse of the earth, the warmth and nourishment of natural surroundings, that ask so little and give so much, rather than a transplanted flower that is growing unhealthfully out of its native soil.

Rather life, I think, than a semblance of Life!

Rather poverty accepted gracefully than riches at the price of health and happiness!

For, after all, money is a hollow thing unless it is buying a dream. And dreams are so priceless that when one is living a dream, money ceases to figure. Dreams cannot be bought.

It has always seemed to me so pitiful a thing to see a man mastered by a thing, rather than a master of things.

Deauville, August 10th

It has long been a part of my dreams, so variously described and to be, I suppose, so variously described again and again, to see the Normandy country. Tales of Normandy had, ever, an unaccountable fascination for me, seeing that there is, so far as I know, no Norman blood running in my veins … and yet how do I know? That very point is another theory I have often played with in my mind. People say to me, to one another: "What *is* an artist?" What is it that makes a man or a woman an artist? It is not birth and breeding, for frequently they spring, these artists, these geniuses, full grown from the barren breasts of poverty; from hovels for homes, from crudity and ugliness and want. It is not country, for the artist arises in darkest Africa and in subtle India. In England and in France. In Germany and in Italy. Everywhere. It isn't training, for many an artist works blindly with his hands and his knowledge, if divinely with his instinct. It isn't luxury; it isn't force of circumstances. It isn't even opportunity. Then what is it? Of what clay is the artist made? What is the spark that kindles him to a flame at which the world may warm its hands?

It may be that the artist is accidentally, oddly, compounded *of all bloods.* It may be that the artist, tracing back and ever back, would find within his veins a diffusion of all traditions; traditions of all lands, heritages of a commingled ancestry, so that he is not merely *one* man, an entity, an individual, with a few subdivisions of ancestry and a few traditions here and there, but the derived essence of all lands and all peoples, hearing the savage tom-tom of the African at the same time as his blood records the symphonies of Boston. He is world-wide, this artist, perhaps; he is the child of the Ages and in him and through him the Ages speak, and all men understand.

I think, perhaps I should say more humbly that I *hope* that I see beauty when and where beauty is to be found. And certainly I know that where and when I find beauty I worship it. Whether it be the beauty of woman, the beauty of nature, or the beauty of mind and soul. But I am not a sentimentalist. Just because a sunset is a sunset, I do not always find it beautiful. I do not always go into raptures and rhapsodies over it. Just because a poem is a poem or a song a song, I do not constantly fold my hands over my chest and sigh, "How marvelous!" And just because a woman is a woman I do not acclaim her with beating heart as a masterpiece from God, a divine acolyte of Venus, a lotus of love. When a woman is beautiful she is a miracle. When she is not beautiful – she is a woman. And her lack is her misfortune. I pity and respect her, but I do not sing Hosannas to her surpassing charm. Truth has beauty, too, it seems to me. Truth of seeing, truth of hearing. Truth of thought.

Juan Les Pins, Nice, August 19th

We had a delicious first day.

One of the really pleasurable excitements of life is getting together in a family group after the group has been separated and dispersed for a considerable period of time.

Natacha's mother and father, "Muzzie" and "Uncle Dick" (Mr. and Mrs. Hudnut), came to Nice a year ago to rebuild and do over the chateau which Uncle Dick had given over to the Government as a hospital during the war. When he retired from business, they came to Nice to settle down largely because it had long been a dream with them to do this very thing.

They had lived on the Riviera off and on for years and always said that when Uncle Dick should have retired from business they would make Nice their permanent home.

It seems to me a fascinating, no, a very satisfactory thing, to have known so well as they did what they wanted to do, where they wanted to go and then to see that dream take size and shape before their very eyes, a dream hewn out of granite and made to live for all who pass to see.

Uncle Dick bought the villa from a Russian prince who had played at Monte Carlo and lost all his money. Natacha and I claimed, as we roamed about the lovely, peaceful grounds, that the fact of this still lingered with the chateau. One could feel somehow about it that tragedies had been lived there, made a little lighter, a little easier to bear because of the sheer beauty of the place. It has marvelous grounds and the sun and air, the sense of peace and beauty must have, I think, calmed the sick terror and distortion in many a poor fellow's riddled heart. I like to think so, at any rate.

I told Natacha that while Muzzie and Uncle Dick might live on the continent, an inalienable part of their hearts and interests would ever rest on American soil. I doubt that anyone can literally expatriate himself or herself. A part of your country remains with you forever, even if the more external signs are never visible. For instance, with me, I look Italian, of course. That is true. But I have more characteristics of Italy than that, even. I don't particularly relish cold weather, for instance. For me shivering and chilling will be, if it ever comes to me, an acquired taste. This is because, I believe, I am born in a tropical climate. For generations, hot suns and fierce suns have penetrated the blood of my forefathers and it has come down to me, still alien to cold.

CHAPTER IV

Valentino died without children. One wonders, after reading the following from his diary, how much heartbreak there was in his childlessness. Certainly, there is little of the "Sheik" in these thoughts.

One hears much ado about the hand that rocks a cradle, but one also hears considerable about the hand that wrecks a home.

It seems to me that the mother in woman is kind, but the female in woman is of the tigress-cat variety, and delights in subtle cruelties, in testing power, in watching the opposite species suffer at her hands.

For it is quite well known that if the maternal in woman be lacking, a sort of monstrosity is the result. Woman may not have any children of their own, perhaps not... but the maternal instinct... the maternal element may be in them very tenderly and very strongly. On the other hand, I have seen women who had children of their own and in whom, I yet missed, felt the lack of the maternal instinct.

Women are not charming unless they have that maternal instinct. They are somehow strangely and lamentably lacking. One misses a vital core to them, which is the only way I can put what I mean.....

Women who cannot be tender, are women to avoid, I believe....They may be kind to you in the flush of success, or while they care about you, but once the emotional afflatus has died down they will turn, snarling, and requite you.... For tenderness is lacking... the fire is built on no sheltering hearth of protectiveness.

I like the Madonna in women... the most beautiful women in Italy are the Madonna type... serene faces ... calm, soft eyes... calm, overlying something deeper and stronger ... mother-women going their ways of beauty and light ... Perhaps my sub-conscious mind, as the psychologists say, received some sort of an impact in early childhood from seeing the Madonna type of beauty in my own land... but I do know that I hark back to it whenever I discuss beauty ... whenever I think of the women of Italy ....

Jaun Les Pins, Nice, August 20th

The third benignant sunny day. Luncheon guests. Talk. It is so nice to feel that so many people are interested in what I do, what I think. I shall never, I believe, recover from the amazement that so many people want to know about what I think, what I plan, what I do from day to day, from week to week.... It is the most stimulating flattery in the world.

Personally, I think the thing to do is to have an all year around home somewhere, as near to ideality as you can find any place. I should like to have such a place, done somewhat in the medieval style. I am not particularly keen for modernity, either in house, dress or woman. I like a touch of the Old World. A flavor of tradition. A hint of other lands and other times... old golds... somber reds... dulled blues... grays that are like smoke drifting.... And I should like to live in such a place, year by year, season following season, so that I should come to know the place, absorb it into myself and be, in turn absorbed into the place.

I have no desire for this flitting from house to house, from estate to estate, never really making a home, an abiding place of any one of them. Never building a tradition.

I should like to *know* my house, to make a shrine of it, where all the beautiful things I am able to garner from the four corners of the globe would find abiding places. Where my friends might come to remember me, as permanently fixed on a "set" at last, and where I might die, at last, after the storm and stress.

It came over me then, in one of those overwhelming moments we are all, I suppose, prone to now and then, how sad it is that the race of man lives as they do live. With a world, sun flooded and sweet with flowers, with garden spots and what the Americans call "the great open spaces" stretching like Edens around and about us, why do we huddle and struggle in cities, wearing our brains and bodies out in the endless struggle for breads and rent and raiment and the pleasures that are like fitful fevers in the end?

But if ever my belief in myself should utterly fail me. If the day should come when my struggle for my individual Right should wear me threadbare of further effort, then I should come to a garden place where the sky would ever be blue above me, where my feet would press soil as vernal and virgin as I could find, where, below me, under white cliffs, the sea could sing me its immemorial lullaby.

I think, there must, at one time or another, have been sailors in my family. For the sea pounds in my veins with a tune I still remember … and I know that I could not have remembered it in this life I have lived.

I extricate myself with some difficulty from this musing in the sun … a place in the sun … a place in the sun … a place in the sun. I have always rather loved the sound of that phrase – it seems to me to sum up in a few words the ultimate philosophy of happiness and peace. What could, after all, be more desirable? Not castle walls nor turreted mansions, nor the velvet-shod ways of the rich … a place in the sun is the birthright of every man and woman… it is the heritage of the race … and each of us could gain it if he would but keep in mind that hope is a grail and a goal ….

There was something very close and beautiful, very dear and intimate between my mother and father. I think it was one of the true loves of the world, one of the dearest married loves it has ever been my privilege to see. In fact, if I have any idealism concerning marriage, and the one, the great, the lasting love (and I have), I owe it to that early example of the existence of such a thing.

If I ever become the artist I hope to be, I shall owe it not so much to my hours of song and dance, as to the many, many hours I have sat alone, friendless, hopeless, hungry of soul as well God knows, as hungry of body.

There is I believe a silver lining to every cloud. But first to our gaze must appear the leaden, lowering cloud in order that we may be the more joyously dazzled by the shining silver underneath.

If we could all realize, *really* realize suffering as, not a thing apart, a thing to be avoided and run from as from isolated things, a pestilential plague, we would be able not only to endure pain more stoically, but we would also grow in nature, mentally and spiritually.

Life is a great travail. Like the flowers who push their valiant way through the dark encumbering earth, often bruised, often, I venture to say, despairing, finally to reach perfection and sweetness under the sun by day and the silver moon by night so most humans push and force their several ways through the dark, encumbering hours before they may attain their measure's growth…

There is probably no worse ordeal given to the long-suffering race of man than the ordeal of waiting. Especially when you are waiting for someone long and eagerly anticipated. Someone whom you have particularly longed to see. Each minute is an hour. Each hour a day. Each day a small eternity.

Apprehensions make the dragging hours tedious. This may have happened, or this … or that … by the time the waiting is well on its way, the one who is waiting, has the expected party dead and buried, and is really in the dour weeds of mourning.

Milan

But, for instance, I'd ask for a bottle of mineral water. There is no ice and the water is served in bottles, which requires that you search about for a bottle opener, if you do not happen (which I do not), to have one hanging on your fob! Then, after you do open the bottle, you find it almost hot. And bad. Very bad. Result: It has taken about an hour to get the water bad, with no ice, and hot as it can be. They have no idea at all of speed, comfort and service. Don't know the meaning of it.

I have often pondered upon the beauty of leisureliness. But I find that leisureliness, like most things, is comparative. It is all right when you want it, and quite the damnable reverse when you don't want it. And one of the times when you most decidedly don't want it is when you are summoning to your side food or drink.

I try, have always tried, NOT to be Rudolph Valentino in the various roles I have played. To do that would be like playing the same tune over and over on the same instrument. However marvelous the piano, or the violin, however exquisite and consummate the tune played, an audience would soon tire of it. Adaptability … versatility … pliability … sensitivity … all of these things are important in the make-up of the artist who must give birth to successive personalities.

I am not afraid of the dead, or of ghosts. The whole store and lore of grisly fears that have shaken the human race at thought or apprehension of meeting with the dead, is quite foreign to me. I am not afraid of anything pertaining to the life beyond.

And it isn't because I don't believe in it. It is because I *do. I believe in the supernatural.* But I don't believe that there is anything I would, or could, be afraid of.

It seems to me that we have more cause to be afraid of the living than of those who have gone on, shaking off, as they go, the lusts and cruelties of the body.

I believe extraordinarily in supernatural manifestations, although I, personally, have never seen any. I am a great believer in the immortality of the soul. That is absolutely beyond any doubt. There must be some ultimate destination or purpose for us.

I know that there has been a lot of fake surrounding Sir Arthur Conan Doyle's experiments, but undoubtedly and all the same, it is a fact that there is something within ourselves, not an organ, which we call a soul, and which cannot cease to live simply because our bodies cease to be active.

What this is we can't tell—until we reach there. And why should we tell? We don't *know* that there is any Tomorrow. Yet we believe that there is, implicitly. And we go on planning for it, although we have no tangible proof that the intangible fact of another Dawn will ever amaze the world, let alone our individual selves.

Our bodies are merely shells, in which we can hear, if we listen with ears attuned, the everlasting murmur of the sea.

What the average man calls Death, I believe to be merely the beginning of Life itself. We simply live beyond the shell. We emerge from out of its narrow confines like a chrysalis. Why call it Death? Or, if we give it the name of Death, why surround it with dark fears and sick imaginings?

I am not afraid of the Unknown.

If you live according to your conscience (if you have one, that is) and you go on through life living according to the dictates of that conscience, in other words, never doing anything which you might yourself be forced to question in discomfort, what is there to fear? What else, what more, can you do? By this I do not mean so much living in the religious sense of the word as living rightfully, living squarely. Not only so far as other people are concerned, but so far as you, yourself are concerned.

A life lived in this way has no dark corners in which ghosts can hide. And a life lived like this would need to have no fear of ghosts seen, then, but the strong, free light of the day. There would be no reason then to fear ghosts any more than the man who is living rightfully has any fear of a policeman. He is afraid, the criminal, because the policeman represents the Law, and in a way the criminal doesn't know what the Law is going to do to him, what it is capable of doing to him. He imagines all sorts of things that he wouldn't and couldn't imagine if his conscience were clear.

I suppose that if I saw a ghost walking about I would be momentarily nervous, not so much because I had seen a ghost, as because I had seen something surprising and new. Something concerning which I have heard, as all have, so many shuddering things. But I feel sure that after the first shock it wouldn't frighten me. It would surprise me as anything would that comes as a shock, but after the shock had worn off, I would get used to it. I might even be able to engage in a pleasant and interested conversation.

Because what would I have to fear from it? Why should I fear? Why should I not rejoice, rather, that I had been privileged to see the ultimate evidence of some life to come after this one has passed away? I'd be a darn sight more afraid of meeting some live person, like an assassin or thief, or something of the sort, in a dark corner, than I would a ghost. I would know the assassin's bad intentions. He would mean to do me harm, and would probably succeed.

People frequently say to me that married couples should separate now and then. For esthetic reasons, I suppose they mean. But I don't agree with them. If harmony is established in marriage, separation disturbs it rather than increases it. And only when the good of one or the other is involved should a separation take place. It is human nature to be lonely, and it is human nature to try to alleviate loneliness by one means or another. It is that very factor that does disturb so many stage and screen and other professional marriages. It is not that the people involved are any more or less fine than other people in other walks of life, but only that they are, perhaps, more sensitive and more highly keyed in conjunction with the fact that the exigencies of their work, not their desires, frequently place them where they are.

Cities have beauty that is as marvelous as the beauty of the countrysides to me. They are enchanted spots if you see them with your eyes half closed. Pinnacles, towers and turrets, opalescent and serene, piercing the very skies with a kind of daring and courage that is breath-taking. They are none the less majestic because they are man-made, for they are born of towering dreams and inspired, even though unconsciously, by the turrets of high mountains, the lift of rock foundations, the sweep of ancient pyramids.

I spent pleasant days with my brother, my sister-in-law and my little nephew, for whom I predict a career either in the cinema or in cars. He seems to lean slightly toward the cars right now, but may change with age. His agility should land him somewhere certainly. He can get over more ground in the shorter space of time and with less apparent effort, than any other human being I have ever noticed, unless it might be Douglas Fairbanks at his best....

But as night approached, there was a gorgeous sunset, and a huge orange moon arose, as huge as a house, so we felt somewhat repaid and calmed for the pains we were taking.

However, irritating and aggravating as a dusty, fretful day may be, I defy any man or woman with so much as the germ of beauty within, to remain chafed and fretted when a moon like saffron silk rises above a land as purple as deep iris. There is something, too, in the air of night, rising out of the ground, that holds a nectar of soothing and sleep. Little things fade away and are lost in the silver shot immensities...

It has become customary in these modern days to laugh, or to pretend to laugh, or to try to laugh at all of the old traditions. The Young Intellectuals poke scoffing fingers at the Old Home, at each and every one of the ancient institutions. Motherhood, the gods of our fathers, tender ties, gently held associations, all of those things have gone out with hoop skirts and golden oak furniture. The two preceding generations have become targets for the skepticism and mockery of this generation of iconoclasts.

Well, it may be all "hokum." There may be "nothing to it." And I may be only a "victim" of past scenes and memories. But I know that a lump rose in my throat and a film crossed my eyes as I pointed out to Auntie the square, flat-roofed farmhouse built of heavy white stone—the house where I was born. I was even guilty of showing her the shuttered windows of the very room wherein that epochal event had miraculously taken place!

I can laugh at it, but the laughter is not altogether free of a softer sentiment. And I am not ashamed of it. He who cannot be stirred is in process of dying, emotionally, if no other way. I remember so well the ceremony of closing those casement windows and barring them at night. The spot where I spent my childhood was not policed as are the suburbs of America, making it neither feasible, nor entirely safe, to leave one's windows open to the night....

When the day for the examinations arrived in the Royal Naval Academy at Venice, I arrived, self-confident and anticipating triumph – only to find myself one inch lacking in chest expansion.

I wanted to die. I felt that I had drunk the very dregs of humiliation. I was tragically convinced that there was no place in the world for such as I. I had ousted myself from my world of dreams and the world of reality would have none of me. It was a bitter, an abysmal moment....

And thus it followed that I went to the Royal Academy of Agriculture to study scientific farming. Italy needed scientific farmers more than she needed sailors and soldiers, my mother said, thus replacing in me the enthusiasm of an ideal which I felt that I had lost for all time for want of an inch. Besides, she reminded me that my illustrious ancestors had tilled the soil of their estates and perhaps I might recreate the traditions, once glorious, of my progenitors. Wise, wise little mother of mine. She touched the quivering strings of my heart and drew forth a whole new harmony. She gave me inspiration and she awakened my determination. I couldn't fail her now, not after the loyal delicate way in which she had stood by me. And so I started to this Agricultural School, of which I have already written, with a high resolution. I wouldn't fail this time. And I didn't....

The utterances of youth are usually bumptious in their effect. Their immediate effect. But I think now that if I ever have a son of my own I will listen to his youthful pronouncements with interest as well as amusement. I will try to recognize in them the clarion call of prophecy. The exaggerated expression of the moment may well be the cornerstone of future activity. Many of the sayings of young boys are mere chaff, of course, not all to be taken seriously, but among the chaff there is frequently to be found the grain of wheat that will mean the harvest of the future man.

The thought and impulse to go to America became so strong within me that I finally communicated it to my mother, and she very naturally was overwhelmed with a sense of the impending loss.

My cousin said: "Let him go. It will do him good. Either make him or break him. And I am sure it will make him if he has any backbone. He will be where he has to fight for his own existence, and will learn to know life. Here he will be absolutely ruined. If he is going to be a criminal, he had better go to America and be one there, where he will not disgrace us and his name."

These family councils – how many young men can look back and remember them. The male members of the family all arguing to let the wastrel go and be broken or made. The mother hanging back, tremulous, fearful, her son's safety of more concern to her than the splendid process, the heartbreaking fear of his being made – or broken. It is the Gethsemane of motherhood, this fear … my mother, being wise, knew that I should certainly get away from the inert, demoralizing influence of the small town. She knew that I wanted to go and that my wanting to get away was the augury of my manhood. But she knew, too, that the odds were against me rather than for me. America was a very long way off – and did she also know that she and I would never meet again on earth? Was that a part of the fear that tore her courage into the little pieces she so valiantly pieced together for my good. I often wonder about that. I so often hope that wasn't a part of what she must have suffered. But I am afraid that it was. Brave little mother, brave mothers the world over, who break their hearts and then say to their sons, "Have you hurt yourselves, my sons?"

The only thing I find that I want, however, is some certainty that my mother knows – she would be proud of me, I think. And I would like her to know that some of her faith, at least, has been justified. Not all, *that* I could never repay, but enough for her to feel that she was not wholly wrong about me. My belief in the life to come gives me, too, the happy conviction that she *does* know and is glad about it all.

It was my mother who got together the money for me to go. It was my mother who talked to me, putting not only new courage, but new ideals into my heart. If, in the days that followed, my courage ever flagged and I felt like giving up the fight, it was my mother's words that buoyed me up, squared my shoulders and made me try again, when trying seemed a futile, worthless thing.

But part of my code has always been that only a coward dies by his own hand, the man worth while hangs on though he hangs to a cross. *I had to hang on.*

More than ever I am eager to work again. More than ever before, I think, I feel all of my capacities at flood tide. There is nothing quite like the upsurging of the desire to do one's chosen work. It is of the very essence of creation. It is the very essence of creation. It is the veritable stuff of which creativeness is made. Writers feel it, poets, artists, artisans, too, I suppose. For all of us are artisans, laboring with our particular materials, each of us as much as an artist as we feel ourselves to be.

It is said that no man is greater than his Art, and I believe that to be true. As a matter of fact, I have often thought that many men are less than their Art.

That they are but vessels of more or less ordinary clay through which the precious essences of Art are poured.

The relation between an artist and his art is always difficult in a curiously special way. Not only must one's mind and spirit be poised and serene – as I feel mine to be now – but material things must be in order before one can give the best that is within him. There must not be baffling and nerve-irritating petty considerations in the way. They, more than any other cause, stultify and retard any really worth-while creativeness.

Home again.
In New York again.

I feel like a schoolboy, like throwing my cap (if I wore one) into the air and shouting "Hurrah! Hurrah!"

The day after I last wrote in my diary we steamed into the harbor, sighting the Statue of Liberty. I must say that no woman, saving my wife, ever looked more beautiful to me. She seemed to me to have a message, especially for me. A message of triumph.

And there, on the dock, was the same official, policeman, who had waved me the lusty good-bye when I sailed. It was like a perfect circle being completed. He had seen me off. He now greeted me in. It gave me a sense of permanency. Of the establishment of all things.

I am at work again.

I am to do the story I have wanted to do for a long, long while.

I am to make "Monsieur Beaucaire."

And so very shortly now I shall go to work. The synopsis has been decided upon, the cast has been decided upon, the cast is about to be assembled, the whole wheels of production are being set in motion and before very long I shall get out the old make-up boxes, the costumes have got to be ordered and selected very carefully, which is going to mean another hasty run across to London, and we shall be ready!

CHAPTER V

It is safe to say that there has never been a star of the screen who has won a following so varied and so loyal as that of Valentino. I have set down here daily occurrences at his tomb, just as they happened, as nearly as I can remember them. In the stories which some of the people tell, it is impossible to separate fact from fancy. Doubtless the two are so mingled in the teller's own mind that one is as real as the other. But in the great majority of these visitors is a simple and homely sincerity. They are neither romantic nor extravagant in the expression of their feeling. Of such was the man with the artificial flowers.

There are times in the winter months, when it rains, that the mausoleum becomes very lonely. It is like a man marooned on an island, waiting for some ship to come, somebody to talk to. This was a day like that, rainy, with the wind howling and getting colder as the afternoon advanced. I had just finished sealing a crypt front to which I had attached a bronze name plate. I was putting my tools away when I happened to glance up.

Along the corridor, almost like a shadow, walked a tall, spare man with stooped shoulders. He was headed in the direction of Valentino's resting place. I followed him. I could see he was wet to the skin, for the trousers clung to his legs. His suit was thin and worn, and on his head was a slouch felt hat with the brim drooping down all around it. He walked to the small corridor which leads to Rudy's crypt and stopped and turned as he heard me approach.

"Good afternoon," he said with a smile, "or should I say, bad afternoon?" and his smile broke into a wide grin.

He seemed a pretty nice sort of fellow, and I smiled in return as I answered, "It's a bad and a good afternoon for me, for I am glad that you came in. It was getting mighty lonesome here among the dead."

He asked if Valentino was near, and I showed him the crypt. I may say here that one amazing fact is the certainty with which total strangers to the mausoleum will more unerringly in the direction of Valentino's resting place. They will get close to it before they ask me where it is. Through thousands of experiences, I know, almost as soon as men or women enter if they are seeking Valentino. So it was with this man.

As we stood before it, he took off his hat and reached up to place his hand on the cold marble. He stood with head bowed, as if saying a prayer. After a while he put his hand inside his wet coat and drew forth a small bunch of artificial flowers. Their colors, of varied tints and shades, were so realistic that they looked like a bunch of wild flowers which had just been picked from some hillside or valley. He looked at me and asked –

"Is it alright if I put them there in one of his vases? I made them myself. I brought them all the way from Toronto, Canada, and I have tried to keep them intact."

I nodded permission, and he placed them in one of the vases. He then went on to tell me his story.

"The depression hit me when I was almost on my feet after a serious illness. It caught me and knocked me back again into the clutches of poverty and sickness. You see, I had been in the war, and the gas kinda stayed with me. I went to making things out of paper and wood fiber, and sold a few and managed to keep going. It was while I was working at my bench at home that I noticed a newspaper article stating that Valentino was forgotten and that no one put flowers at his crypt any more. It struck me as pretty bad, for I had always admired him, and saw all his pictures. I wondered how all his friends could so soon forget. So I made a lot of flowers and determined that I would some day journey to Hollywood and put them at his crypt.

I knew that I would have to go for a desert climate soon for my health. Each day I saved a little. Finally I had enough to last me until I could find some work. As luck would have it, I read in a States newspaper where a company wanted a man to be caretaker of a small ranch in Arizona. I telegraphed them immediately, and they wired back for me to report by the first of February. I still have a few days in which to get there. These flowers are all I have left of the ones I made…. I am surprised to find flowers in his vases. It is not true, then, what the newspapers printed?"

I told him no, that Valentino had flowers the year round. I pointed to a large basket beneath the crypt. "That basket is always full of flowers. There is a Valentino association in England that takes care that he shall always be remembered."

"Well, that's fine!" he exclaimed. "But could you, when his vases are empty, put mine in them? I want to do my part for Mr. Valentino. I always liked him – in fact, idolized him. I came almost five hundred miles out of my way just to do my part and to see with my own eyes whether he was cared for or not."

He said he had to go, and we bid each other good bye. I watched him go into the rain, a tall thin man with a suggestion of the soldier he had been in his now squared shoulders and confident step.

Magazine and newspaper articles came out with the statement that Valentino was lying in Mr. Balboni's crypt and that, if something was not done about it, his remains would be taken out and buried in a pauper's grave. This, of course, brought me many letters and personal inquiries asking if it were true. Now, when Valentino died, June Mathis, who was Mr. Balboni's wife, gave Alberto, Rudy's brother, permission to use her crypt as a temporary vault. It was to be used until the Valentino family could build or select a permanent place for Rudy's body. But a year later June herself died, and Rudy's body was transferred to the crypt adjoining, which was owned by Mr. Balboni. There it lay, waiting for the Valentino estate to be settled. Finally Mr. Balboni sold it to the estate. Rudy now has his own crypt. And he is well remembered with flowers the year round. On last Decoration Day (1937) there were at least 4000 visitors at his tomb.

Among those who came one day, several years ago, was a delightful little lady who informed me proudly that she was eighty years old and a great-grandmother. She wanted to buy the crypt directly over Valentino. But when I told her that he might be moved later on, as he was merely occupying a section of the June Mathis group, she decided not to buy.

"He was so sweet," she said. "I loved him like one of my own children. If I cannot be near him always here, I will wait awhile until they decide where he is to be moved. Then perhaps it can be arranged."

Once, while I was on my vacation a woman about forty-five years old came to the mausoleum. She asked the attendant, who was taking my place, the where-abouts of Rudy's crypt.

She requested that she be left alone there, as she wished to communicate with Rudy's spirit if possible. She went on to say that she was a medium and had talked with Rudy many times in her own home, but that he had always disappeared before she had the opportunity to ask him as many questions as she wished. She therefore had come to the cemetery that she might better converse with him.

The attendant left and a short time later the lady came running to him, and cried, "Come quick, Rudy knocks! Rudy knocks!"

She grabbed him by the arm, all excited, and together they ran to Rudy's crypt. Sure enough, a tapping could be heard from above. By this time other people who were in the mausoleum came to find out what the excitement was. They too heard the knocking. Many of them believed that Rudy was tapping a message to the medium.

The attendant quietly left the group and, with an assistant, crawled up into the attic. Making their way to the place where the tappings were, they found a large bird caught in the air vent. They soon freed it and went back to tell the people at the crypt the cause of the tappings.

The face of the medium turned all colors. She said she was sorry that she had caused all the commotion. The other people laughed and made so much fun of her that she left in a hurry.

I can picture him yet as he stood before Rudy's crypt, a well tailored young man in the latest sport clothes. Dark, good looking, he stood there with two little daisies in his hand, flowers he had picked from the cemetery lawn. Love and Devotion he told me, was what they meant. He placed them on the ledge of the crypt and added:

"I am a tailor and rather psychic. Oftentimes, when I am at work, spirits have such a strong influence on me that I go where they direct. Valentino called me today, and here I am. I picked the flowers under his spell, and he bade me place them at his tomb as love and devotion for his admirers. I have done as he directed. My task is finished. I must go now, back to my work. That is where the spirits find me. Why, I cannot tell."

He bid me good-bye and sauntered leisurely out of the mausoleum. I saw him again after that, but I was busy conducting a funeral and did not have a chance to talk with him.

While many attractive women come to pay homage at Rudy's crypt, there is one of exceptional beauty. A sweet, wistful face under a crown of gorgeous blonde hair, large eyes and the longest eyelashes I have ever seen. Lips like red roses.

She walked into the mausoleum with the grace of a deer. She carried a small rabbit, cuddled in her arms. Approaching me she asked, "Is there some water, so that I may give my bunny a drink? We have come a long way and I know he must be thirsty." I brought water and both refreshed themselves.

Then, to my surprise, she said, "You must be the man I dreamed about, over a month ago. Yes, you are the image of him. I had a horrible dream. I was walking along a high cliff, I had the feeling that I must get down somehow. There were steps, but the height made me dizzy. Then came that dreadful feeling one has at times when looking down from a great height; the urge to jump came to me. As I was about to leap into space, out of the shadows came Rudolph Valentino riding a great white horse. He spoke to me, and how his words cling in my memory. He said, 'Do not destroy that which is beautiful. God has given you life for you to live. Fear not the future. Your life has been a lesson; carry on and profit by your experiences. The greatest goal is true love. Look and you shall see. Fear not to go down those steps. A man who watches my place of rest will meet you and see that you will be safe.' With those words he was gone. My mind seemed to become clear; the steps deemed larger and safer, and as I started down, who should I see but a large man, dressed just as you are, looking just as you do. I gave him my hand, and it seemed as if we went down that dreaded flight of steps in perfect safety. I awoke and remembered the words of Valentino about the man who guarded his resting place, so I decided to go and see if dreams really have a meaning – and here I am. This is the greatest adventure I have ever undertaken – trying to solve a dream, and succeeding. Please show me Valentino's tomb."

Still astonished at the whole thing, I led her to the crypt. She made a beautiful picture as she stood facing it. Her figure, outlined against the stained glass window, seemed to be part of it.

I walked softly away. In a few minutes she came to where I was, down the corridor, and thanked me for my attention. She said she was leaving for Chicago the following day to meet her husband, a Count. She showed me newspaper clippings containing pictures of herself and her husband. Since then she has come to the mausoleum several times while on trips to Hollywood.

There was nothing flirtatious, nothing silly about her. I have found her to be thoroughly sincere, cultured and well balanced. So this is another episode that leaves me wondering. Did the spirit of Valentino guide her to me? She has repeatedly said that the description of the man in the dream was I, in size, appearance, and dress.

On a marble ledge, just above Valentino's crypt, is a penny. It was placed there by a young man from St. Louis. Because it is above the level of the eye, no one has seen it, so it has been safe from the souvenir hunters. It lies just where it was put, nearly two years ago.

He was a slender man of about thirty-five years. I found him on his knees at Valentino's crypt. I waited until he arose before I made my presence known.

He said as he looked up, "I have been saying a prayer for Rudy. I hope you do not mind."

I assured him that it was all right, and he went on: "I have just arrived from St. Louis and this is one of the first places I wanted to visit. I have a sister back home who is as great an admirer of Valentino as I am. We used to see all his pictures. My sister has read in the newspapers and magazines about visitors who come from all over the world to pay their respects here. When she found out I was coming to California she made me promise to see Valentino's tomb. She gave me a penny and said for me to place it on or as near Rudy's crypt as possible. She thinks it will bring me good luck in my search for employment, and also serve as a remembrance from her. Is there somewhere near the crypt here, that I can put it?"

He was so sincere that I told him to place it on the ledge right over Rudy's crypt. There no one would see it to take it. He thanked me. I gave him some flowers and some beads from a wreath, and told him to send them to his sister. He promised to do so as he bid me good-bye. I wonder how long the penny will remain. Nearly every day I look to see if it is still there.

There were a lot of people here today. One was a girl who came with a party. She had flowers and fixed them very attractively in Rudy's vases. I was standing by her side when she whispered, "Rudy was my sweetheart. He came to me always in my dreams. You are laughing, are you not?" she asked as she caught me smiling.

"No," I said. "Please go on. I would like to hear your story."

"I have come from a long ways, Argentina," she told me. "I was born there, but received my education in London and New York. I met Valentino in a theatre. I had friends who owned this theatre and they invited me to come and see Valentino act. I had a very good seat behind the scenes. I remember when we first met, I blushed and trembled when he looked at me. It was only a short time before he had to go on the stage. He took me to one side. What he told me I cannot tell, but it seemed our feelings were mutual. That is why I come today, to pay my respects." She rearranged the flowers and after touching Rudy's crypt, went away.

A beautiful girl used to come here every Sunday. She would not say a word of who she was. She always brought a potted plant and watered it with her tears, for it seemed she was continually crying.

One day I asked her if I could be of any help. She replied, "Yes. Please take care of the plants that I have here, for I am going away and I may never return." Her blue eyes filled again with tears. I said I would do as she wished, and told her I was sorry to see her cry so much.

"Rudy meant so much to me," she murmured. "I loved him because—because – " Her voice faltered. Again she looked at me. "Because he loved me."

With those words she fell to weeping again. I left her alone. When I returned she was gone. I never saw her again. I will never forget the lonesome look she had.

One cannot judge these characters too harshly, for it is difficult to tell the sincere from the insincere.

One afternoon not long ago, it was my misfortune to lock a man up in the mausoleum. I had noticed him some time earlier, sauntering around, looking at the various names on the niches and crypts. That day had been a busy one, with two funerals and many visitors asking to see Valentino's tomb.

This man was a peculiar sort of fellow. He appeared and disappeared in different places about the mausoleum for an hour or more. I finally caught up with him down at Valentino's crypt and saw him taking some flowers from the vases. I asked him what he was doing. He replied that he was only taking some flowers for souvenirs. He said that he had known Rudy back in New York, when the screen star had first come to America. This was his first visit to Hollywood, and his first sightseeing trip had been to Valentino's resting place.

I made him put the flowers back into the vases and told him that there was a fine for taking flowers from crypts, graves or niches. He seemed frightened at that and offered his apologies. I then gave him a flower. He thanked me and put it into an envelope that he had taken from his pocket.

I left him at the mausoleum entrance while I went to change to my street clothes. When I returned he was gone. I went through the building to see if anyone was still inside. I also called, "All out!" a few times. I saw no one and locked the door.

As I did so, I had an uneasy feeling that I had locked someone inside, but dismissed it as a foolish fancy, since I had looked and called before closing. I locked up another mausoleum of which I have charge and drove toward home.

But, as block after block was passed, some strange inner force seemed to be drawing me back to the cemetery. The feeling became so strong that I finally turned my car around and headed back. As I drove up to the mausoleum entrance, I saw a dozen or more people standing on the steps. They were peering through the windows of the big doors.

When I ran up the steps, they told me that they had heard someone pounding on the doors. "There's a man locked up in there," they said, "and he seems sort of frightened, being locked up with the dead."

I opened the door, and there stood my peculiar visitor, shamefaced and scared. I demanded to know how he got in, and what he was doing.

He confessed in a timid voice, "I sneaked back to get one of Valentino's vases; but you returned and I hid in a small recess by the window. I thought I could get out after you had gone, but the windows were too small. So I'm caught red-handed."

I gave him a lecture and sent him on his way, thankful that whatever it was that had warned me had come in time. It wouldn't have been pleasant for him to have stayed there all night.

OLD FAITHFUL

Although I call her Old Faithful, it does not imply that she is old. She is about forty. As long as I can remember she has come every so often with her small bunch of flowers and placed them at Rudy's crypt.

She was a little shy at first but soon overcame this. We got to be good friends and she told me quite a bit about herself. She said she had seen all of Valentino's pictures and believed he was the greatest actor she had ever seen. She called him, "My boy."

Her husband left her years ago with a small child which she had clung to and raised to manhood. Her hands are gnarled and calloused from doing hard work, and yet she finds time to come many miles out of her way with her meager offering.

Valentino represents all the romance in her life. She went to the studio once to see him work, but was too bashful to ask for an introduction. She says, however, that he glanced her way and smiled while looking directly into her eyes. That moment she will treasure forever. A few weeks later, he left for New York, where he died.

She failed in her endeavor to meet him while he lived and now she spends what time she can by his side in death. The flowers she brings she feels are a pitiful offering as compared to some of the others she sees by his crypt. She furtively slips her few blossoms among the others as though she is ashamed of the home-grown tribute. I know of none that are more sincere.

I'll never forget the time she met Alberto, Valentino's brother. She was busy fixing her small bouquet in Rudy's vases when he appeared. She must have recognized Alberto from his pictures, for she seemed paralyzed by embarrassment. She simply cowed in a corner, as if to hide from him.

I knew she would like to meet him, so I made it a point of introducing them. When I told him how she came regularly to bring flowers, he thanked her graciously. I have never seen anyone so pleased as she was.

It was after that that I gave her the name of Old Faithful, and she seems to rather like the title.

CHAPTER VI

Rudolph Valentino was born in Castellaneta, Italy, May 6, 1895. Originally there were seven words in his name, but when he came to America he shortened it to Rodolpho Valentino. Since Americans persisted in calling him Rudolph instead of Rodolpho, he finally accepted the former name.

When the boy was eleven years old, his father died, and he was sent away to school for the next two years. His high spirits kept him more or less in hot water here, and he was finally expelled. The reason for the expulsion is told with refreshing humor in Valentino's diary. The king was to pass through the town, and, in common with every boy in school, Rudy ardently desired to see his king. But, because of some misdemeanor, he was locked in the dormitory that day. Rudy was by no means defeated, although his situation appeared pretty hopeless by reason of the fact that he had been stripped of most of his clothes when he was locked up. How he broke out, and how he solved the problem of clothing, and by what means he rode to see his king can be fully appreciated only through his own account of the affair.

His next venture in education was at the Royal Naval Academy. He threw himself whole-heartedly in preparation for the entrance examination – and failed only because he lacked an inch in chest expansion. He was profoundly humiliated over this defeat, and decided that life was not worth living.

But his wise and loyal mother persuaded him that there still was hope, and advised his entrance of the Royal Academy of Agriculture. Here he really made good, graduating with highest honors.

But success seemed to be a heady wine, and he went off at a natural, youthful tangent. Nothing would do but that he must go and conquer Paris. His own account of this episode is rich in a keen and delightful humor that is never bitter. In no manner and in no circumstances does he ever spare himself.

After Paris and a foray on Monte Carlo, came the inevitable return home, broke. His family met to consider seriously the problem of the future for this eighteen-year-old boy. His uncle concluded that if he was going to turn out a criminal, he had better be a criminal in far-off America, where the disgrace would not reach his family.

To America he came, with the money his mother had raised for him. Having had no training in the handling of money, he soon went through his. After that he did all sorts of work for a living, some of it back-breaking work, and finally became a dancer. Though he was more than once driven to it, then and always he disliked dancing as a profession. Since his only real success so far had been at the agricultural school, he felt that he should utilize that knowledge. That is what really drew him to California.

In the meantime, war had been declared. Valentino tried to enter the Italian flying service, and later the British. In both cases he was rejected because of poor eyesight.

Next came Hollywood, with its great disappointments and small victories. Many men were kind to him here, notable among them Norman Kerry, who never failed the shy but eager and hopeful boy. After a few small parts in pictures, Rudy was forced to turn to dancing again to make a living. Then came his chance as an Italian "heavy." This and other chances were brought to him by Emmett Flynn, and Valentino was intensely grateful to Flynn for it. He never forgot a kindness from anyone.

His fortune varied in Hollywood for some time, occasionally reaching a moderate high, often hitting a serious low.

Then, through the faith and persistence of June Mathis, he was given the part of Julio in The Four Horseman of the Apocalypse. Thanks to the superb directing of Rex Ingram, Valentino's talent and power, and that mysterious something which we call personality, for lack of a better word, were given full swing.

His difficulty with Famous Players-Lasky began to brew after this, and was the result of Valentino's passion for honesty. He believed in honest work as an artist and absolute square dealing with the public. In this quarrel with the producers, and in other matters he was sometimes misrepresented by the newspapers. Misrepresentation stung him more than most people realized. Intensely sensitive, as any great artist must be, he yet had a streak of iron in his character that would brook no tampering with principles in which he believed.

Prevented by an injunction from acting on stage or screen, he toured the country with his wife, Natacha Rambova, as a dancing partner. It was at this time that he became acquainted with George Ullman, who later became his manager. Ullman, in his biography of the actor, tells of Valentino's ability as an extempore speaker. One night in Montreal, after a speech in English to an enormous crowd, he suddenly realized that this was a bi-lingual town. Whereupon, to wild applause, he repeated almost the entire speech in French.

He commanded at least five languages, possibly more. When one reads the many remarkable passages in his diary, and considers that Valentino knew not one word of English when he landed in New York, there is a strong inclination to agree with the opinion of O.O. McIntyre – "He was a scholar, indeed a poet; and had he used his pen as an Alpine stock, he would have scaled the Matterhorn."

Valentino's comeback on the screen, in Monsieur Beaucaire and some of the pictures that followed, was extraordinarily successful. It proved beyond any doubt that his popularity was based on something real. In this man's dynamic and magnetic personality was a quality which responded to and filled a vital human need. Touched with the romantic, it was much more than romance, deeper and more searching. It still brings mourners to his tomb by the thousands.

As regards Valentino's two marriages, opinions naturally differ. The truth of the Jean Acker episode became known only after Valentino's death. That this fine girl and he were always friends speaks much for the quality of both of them. Valentino's failure to reach the happiness he sought is common enough to the artist, and to the idealistic temperament. Certainly there was a solid core of strength in his character which would have, given the discipline of years and experience, won for him peace, if not happiness.

He was intensely masculine, and of a superb physical development. He kept himself in condition, not only because of the joy he got out of perfect health, but because nothing else would serve the best interests of his work. That he got no pleasure from the appellations of "great lover" and "sheik" was well known among his intimates; but he took it as part of the day's work and was confident that the years, with their opportunity for greater work, would justify him.

Valentino's deep seated sincerity in and for his work, his willingness to labor to the point of exhaustion to achieve a finished product, would have raised him to the top of his profession if Fate had only given him more time. He had an unshakable confidence in himself, and in his ability to reach the high goal he had set. But this self confidence of his could never, by any stretch, be termed conceit. One who knew him well, and is qualified to make the observation, said – "No man I have ever known was quite so humble in success." He was never satisfied with what he had done, would always see a hundred points at which he might have improved upon it.

His self restraint, his good manners, his tenderness for children, the deep kindliness which was a part of him – these traits are described best by those who knew him well. Some of their comments I have quoted elsewhere.

He was quite without fear of any kind. Death itself he took in his stride, as he had taken life.

CHAPTER VII

Soon after Valentino died, two large beaded memorial wreaths were delivered at the mausoleum. One of them was from his good friend Clarence Victor Miller, who had it made in France and brought it over to this country when he came back from abroad. Who gave the other wreath I do not know. I think it was made in Italy and sent by some admirer.

These wreaths are composed of thousands of small beads, which are strung on fine wire and woven into flower designs of various colors and patterns. They were placed at Valentino's crypt and remained there until 1930. I then removed them because they were getting shabby from being mutilated by souvenir hunters. Whenever people express a wish for some token of remembrance of Rudy, I give them a few beads from the wreaths. These little souvenirs are now scattered all over the world.

One afternoon two swarthy turbaned Hindus came into the mausoleum. They inquired about the resting place of a missionary whom they had known in India. I looked for the name they gave, in my book where I keep all my records. I pointed out the crypt and they stood before it and talked to one another in their native tongue.

They finally spoke to me and asked if they could see the resting place of Valentino. I showed them his crypt. They stood before it and, it seemed to me, repeated the same conversation. They asked me a lot of questions about Valentino.

One, whom I judged to be the older, said, "Mr. Valentino was a genius. He created a change in motion pictures, that brought romance to the world and happiness to thousands. May his spirit rest in peace." As he finished, he bowed his head towards Rudy's crypt and murmured a few words. They asked if they would be allowed to take a picture of the crypt. I told them we were not in the habit of doing that; but since they had come so far, it would be all right. They thanked me and took some time exposures. They seemed so interested in Valentino I gave them some of the beads from one of the wreaths. This pleased them immensely. They thanked me again and bid me good-bye.

This young girl came seeking Valentino's tomb. She was just a little thing. In her arms was a dear baby wrapped in a blanket. I asked if I could carry it and she said I could. It was a little girl.

"What a wonderful bunch of happiness you have here," I told her.

"Happiness, you say?" she asked.

I answered, "Yes, a baby like this would bring happiness to anyone." As I looked into her eyes, I could see tears forming. We had reached Valentino's crypt and I did not say any more about the baby. I told her about Rudy, and she asked me many questions concerning the people who come here.

"Does anyone," she wanted to know, "ever have any dreams about him?

I replied, "Yes, lots of them do."

"The reason I asked," she went on, "is because I have dreams about him so often." Then she told a story which I will give as I recall.

"I am seventeen years old and I have had a hard journey in this life so far. I wonder if it is really worth while after all. There is a man," she pointed at Rudy's crypt, "who was at the peak of his career, and death took everything away. As young as I am, I loved him dearly, although I only saw him in pictures. I was born in a sod shanty in Dakota. There the golden wheat grows, the air is fresh and people seem more human. I would give anything if I could go back. I can't go now, not with the baby. You see I am not married. I am one of the girls who came to Hollywood to seek work in the movies. Like many of the others, I fell because I was innocent.

"Why I am telling you this I do not know. Maybe it's because we are in the presence of Valentino. The baby is like a message from God, making me brave to carry on, for she is everything I have left to live for. Were it not for her I would give up trying."

I gave the baby a tug with my finger as I talked with the little mother.

"There is much to live for," I told her. "This baby was put on this earth for a purpose, as you and I were. God only knows what that purpose is. We must live our lives the best we can and profit by our experiences. God is just, and even if the baby wasn't born as you would wish, it is the same as anyone else. My girl, that baby to you is a gift from heaven. It will change your life and teach you to think for yourself."

This little girl went her way and promised me she would write home. She came to me a short time later and said, "Mr. Peterson, I am going home. I have so much to thank you for that I don't know how to begin." She jumped up and kissed me and started to cry. Tears always embarrass me. There was a big lump in my throat. She prepared to leave and I said, "Before you go, may I ask why you wanted to know whether other people ever had dreams about Valentino?"

She looked at me with a wistful smile and answered, "When I was despondent I was going to kill myself and my baby. For three nights I would have a dream about Valentino. He would tell me not to do it. So I just had to think there was something big in those dreams. That is why I came to where he is interred. So you see I have a lot to be grateful for now. I again wish to thank you for what you have done."

She shook my hand. It was a farewell I will never forget. The long shadows of the setting sun reached far out over the graves of the cemetery as she made her way down the road, carrying her little baby. A waif from the open spaces going home.

Never will I forget the day when many of the passengers and crew from the great ship Empress of Britain, paid homage to Valentino. The party drove up in large busses and private cars. When they unloaded and came into the mausoleum, one would have thought that a great funeral was about to take place.

Officers of the ship acted as guides and spokesmen. I knew, before they asked, who it was they sought. I said, "Come this way," and led them to Valentino's tomb.

Many foreign people were in the crowd. Many spoke in their native tongue or in broken English. Some knelt and said a prayer. Others asked if it was all right for them to place their hands on the crypt. I told them it was and suggested that they should stand in line, so that each one could pay homage in his own way. Some such arrangement as this was necessary, with a crowd of two hundred people, because the crypt is situated at the end of a rather narrow corridor.

It was an impressive sight, this orderly, reverent procession, a sight to make one marvel at the strange influence which Valentino held and still holds over thousands. Many wiped away tears as they stood before his crypt. Some would reach up stealthily and pluck a flower. I did not say anything until all had paid homage. Then I told them that if anyone would like to have a flower for a souvenir, he might take one. Those who already had one edged aside, while the others made short work of the remaining blossoms. They were pleased over this privilege, and many shook hands with me and thanked me. They promised to come each year, and have done so.

One of the officers gave me a pass to visit the ship, which was good for as many friends as I cared to take with me. I thanked him and promised to be there at an appointed time.

That visit was a high light in my life. The friends I made there and on subsequent visits to the ship now write to me from different parts of the world. The guardianship of Valentino's tomb has brought me many fine things, and above all I cherish the friendships I have made with his admirers.

A woman of about thirty-five, who was a quarter blood Cherokee, used to be a frequent visitor at the mausoleum.

About a year ago she came dressed in Indian clothes. Around her neck she wore many strings of beads of all colors. Her dress was of leather, fringed with buckskin and decorated with beads and shells. The coat over it, a mass of Indian designs woven from the raw wool, was trimmed with rows of ornaments in hammered copper and silver. Under a brightly beaded tam-o'shanter, her heavy hair hung over her shoulders in two thick braids.

I followed her down the corridor. She seemed to be looking for something. When she saw me she asked if Valentino's remains were in the mausoleum. I pointed the crypt out to her.

"I had a hunch he was down here," she said. "Something inside of me made me come this way. It must be Indian intuition," and she smiled.

I helped her with her flowers and walked away so she could be alone. After a while she motioned for me to come. She asked me many questions concerning Valentino. I answered all of them I could. After that she told me her story.

"I knew Valentino when he was an extra in pictures. I used to own an antique shop in Hollywood and he used to come in and visit when he wasn't working. He got to calling me Mamacita, which means little mother in Mexican. I think he called me that because I helped him when his spirits were at an ebb, for lots of times he wanted to give it all up and go back to Italy. He loved art and he admired beauty of all kinds. He was very religious and used to go to church real often. He would have made a very good priest.

"He used to tell me how he would like to arrange his home, if he had one. He had it all planned in his mind, just how it would be. He loved dogs, and would bring them to my shop and I would feed them. He used to like to cook spaghetti and we had many meals together. He was always buying me beads of brilliant hue, as he knew I had Indian blood and loved bright colors. He gave me his own prayer beads.

"We drifted apart after a while and ever saw one another again. On the day of his funeral I made my way to the cemetery. There were many people and I had difficulty getting near, so I asked an actress if she would take my flowers, which she did.

"I sold my business and went east on a visit. When I returned I went to the cemetery to pay my respects to Rudy, but I did not know where he was laid away. I thought it was the mausoleum on the island, so I went there and offered a prayer, and placed my flowers at the door. I left his rosary hanging from a tree near the mausoleum and I believe it is still there. Let us go and see."

We made our way to the island, which is in the center of a lovely little lake. Sure enough, there was the rosary, dark and rusted, hanging on a cypress tree. When we had returned to the mausoleum she asked if she could leave it on Valentino's crypt. I told her it would not last long there, as someone would surely carry it off for a souvenir.

"You take it then," she said, "and keep it as a remembrance of Rudolph." I thanked her, for I was indeed grateful. She came many times after that and often brought other Indians with her. Their attitude was always reverent.

He was just a little fellow, as Chinese go, and when he came into the mausoleum looking for the resting place of Valentino he appeared timid and uncertain. He asked me in perfect English if he could see Rudy's tomb, and I directed him to it.

He gazed at the bronze marker that bore Rudy's name, then slowly stepped forward and placed both of his hands on the plaque. With head bowed, he stood motionless for some time.

I left and returned shortly to find him taking a picture of the crypt with a small camera. He tried to hide it as I approached; but I told him it was all right. He thanked me and said he wanted a picture for his wife in China.

"Why," I exclaimed, "I didn't know the people of China were interested in Valentino."

He smiled as he said, "In China we have many theatres, and people there are very fond of motion pictures. Valentino was the favorite of all the stars; and the theatre was always packed when a picture of his was shown."

He had seen all of Valentino's pictures in China and gone to see them again while at school in America. It was seeing Valentino on the screen for the first time that changed his life. It made him want to see this country and to get a foreign education. He had read about how Valentino had come to America to seek his fortune and had made good. This young Chinese determined to do likewise.

He told me how he had worked and saved his money. With the help of a rich uncle, he had finally managed to gain entry to this country, where he could better his education. The going was hard in this strange land, and many times he felt like giving up and returning home. When he got in these moods he would remember Valentino, and if possible see one of his pictures. That would give him the will to see through.

Now, he was on his way back, and he thought it fitting that he should pay his respects, before he departed for his home land. There, he said, he was assured of an excellent position with the government.

"That man's spirit," he said, and pointed to Rudy's crypt, "is my guiding star. It has led me on. I shall always remember that, and cherish his memory."

I gave him some flowers and a few beads from the wreath. He then bid me good-bye and went out of the mausoleum, his head back and shoulders set, ready to face the world.

A girl came in one day and asked for a rose from Valentino's tomb. She was a visitor from Chicago and was going back in a few days. She told me that her employer had visited the mausoleum the year before and had brought back a rose. He gave a petal from it to every girl in the office. The gift had been so greatly prized by the girls that this young lady had been made to promise that she would attempt to get another rose when she came to California.

She was a very attractive girl and always had a friendly smile. She brought large yellow roses and placed them in the vases. Then she stood in a corner and watched the other visitors come and go. If they left flowers, she would take a blossom or two and put in a brief case she always carried with her.

She came every day for a week and always brought roses. If there were flowers there, she would take a few blossoms as before. The last day she came, she said –

"It has been wonderful to visit here and see the people pay homage to Rudy. It is an experience I never will forget. The girls in the office will be envious of me when I tell them. I have enough blossoms for all of them, and they will be so pleased to think they have souvenirs right from Rudy's crypt. My vacation is over and I must hurry back. Some day, if fortune favors me, I shall come back to stay. For it is so nice here in California."

She thanked me for my courtesy towards her and said good-bye.

One of the weirdest cases that has come under my observation here in the mausoleum is that of a little lady who came to the cemetery in the late fall of 1930. I can still see her as she came trudging up the road.

As she approached where I stood, I saw she was a nice looking woman of thirty-five or so. The one striking feature about her was her eyes, which were at once restless and staring, if such a thing can be.

She asked to be shown to Rudy's crypt. When she reached there, she kissed the marble front of the crypt fervently, murmuring words of love with passionate abandon. I did not like to be present at such a spectacle so I tiptoed away.

After some time, she joined me in another part of the mausoleum and told me of the warning she had received before the death of Valentino. As near as I can remember, I will tell the story as she told it to me.

"About two months before Valentino died, I had three dreams on three different nights. On the first night I dreamed I was walking in the beautiful grounds of a large castle situated on the banks of a rushing little river. As I walked, a flood of light was thrown about the tower of the castle and I could see a man pacing about inside, occasionally stopping to peer between the bars of the huge windows. I hurried to the base of the tower and tried to make out who the man in captivity was, but I was unable to distinguish his features.

"When I awoke, I was very much troubled as I realized that it meant evil to someone. I told my friends about it, but they laughed and told me to forget it.

"On the second night, I dreamed again of the castle, but this time the lights were much stronger about the tower, and the man looked longer through the bars. Then I recognized the features as those of Rudolph Valentino. I had dreamed of him many times before, but not a dream with evil portent as this seemed to be.

"I awoke quickly after recognizing the man, but I was wet with perspiration, and suddenly I fainted. My husband revived me and asked me what had caused me to faint. I told him, and he laughed at me and tried to assure me that my fears were groundless, as did my friends when I repeated the occurrence to them. But in my heart I felt that something terrible was going to happen to Valentino, and I was powerless to stop it.

"On the third night I was loath to go to bed, and sat around for hours dreading the moment I would dream. But at last I became so weary that I fell asleep in my chair, and found myself again in the castle garden. And again I saw Rudy walking back and forth, back and forth, pausing occasionally and peering through the window as though searching for someone.

"Then out of the darkness above the tower a white horse with nostrils gleaming and surrounded by a halo of fire, galloped up to the tower. The walls of the tower separated and allowed the beast to pass within. In a moment, the animal, with Rudy on his back, emerged and made straight for where I was standing. I jumped aside to allow it to pass. As I did this, Rudy took a rose, a red one, from his girdle, kissed it and threw it to me. In a moment horse and rider disappeared in the distance, and I awoke.

"I was crying as though my heart would break, and I told my husband that Rudy was going to die. He told me I was foolish and to get in bed and go to sleep, but I could not sleep any more. That dream was too vivid. I told the girls at the factory where I worked, too. But they also laughed at me.

"It was only a few days later, however, that one of the girls returned from lunch and said, "Rose, your dream has come true. Valentino died this noon!

"My heart was broken. I became so ill that I had to be taken home. I hurried here to Hollywood, to be near him when he was laid away. Although there were thousands milling about the cemetery, I managed to make my way into the mausoleum, and was fairly near the casket as it was brought in. As the procession passed me, a big rose fell from the blanket of flowers which covered his coffin and landed right at my feet.

"I picked it up, and I have it pressed between the leaves of my Bible. Remembering the episode of the flower in my dream, it seems that I had received a gift from Rudy himself. But I never will be the same since he went away. I am lonely for him night and day."

I felt sorry for the woman as she ended, but I am forced to admit that her story sounded a little far-fetched.

A short time after this, the same woman returned with a potted plant which she placed near the Valentino crypt. On the third day, the little lady returned and found the plant withered and dead. She stared with those uncanny eyes as she told me:

"All day I have been under a spell. I consulted a medium, and she told me that Rudy was earthbound and calling me. She said that if the plant which I had left was withered today, I probably would not live long."

She spread her fingers apart in a gesture of resignation. "You have seen the plant," she continued. "It would seem that I am under a strange power and am not long for this life. If I am not able to return, I will bid you farewell."

With these words, she left the mausoleum, and I have never seen her since.

One old Italian with gnarled fingers and a weather beaten face, dropped on his knees in front of Valentino's crypt and crossed himself as he said his prayers.

When he arose, there were tears in his eyes as he spoke in broken English, "He was a gooda man, a gooda Italian man. He die too young. Everybody like him. Me, I go to see every picture he make. I feel very proud when I see him in the Sheik. He maka love justa like me!"

His face lit up with a cheery smile.

"I gotta boy. He looka just like Rudy, and I tell him why don't he try and get in pictures? But I don't know. He no gotta pep, just smoke cigarettes and stay out late at night. I think I take him to see Mr. Warner Brothers. Maybe we get the contract, make gooda money and then maybe I go back to Italy to see my wife."

I could not help but smile at him, for he seemed so sincere. It wasn't long after that he returned with his boy. The latter, I must say, looked more like Bull Montana than Valentino. It was interesting to see these two in front of Valentino's crypt, talking in Italian and broken English. It soon became so loud I had to quiet them. As they left the mausoleum they seemed to muttering threats at one another.

Four years after Valentino's death and on his anniversary, August 23, I met a beautiful girl. I think she was German. I can see her yet as she walked into the mausoleum and asked for Valentino's crypt. I told her how to get there and then I went and got a basket for her flowers.

As I drew near to where Rudy lies I could hear singing. I saw her standing there, silhouetted against the stained glass window. She made a beautiful picture. When she saw me she stopped. I found out later that she had written a poem and it was this which she was singing before the tomb.

I helped her with the flowers and found her a chair so that she might rest awhile.

"I am glad," she said, "to see him have so many flowers today. He deserves them, for he has given us a lot of things to be thankful for. Do you know, I met Rudy in Westlake park over eight years ago. It was mutual love at first sight and we had a grand time sitting there in the park. He told me then that he had hopes of being a star some day.

"I used to bring a basket of lunch and when we were finished eating we fed the birds with what we had left over. Soon after, I lost track of him because I had to return to Milwaukee, for my mother was ill. I never saw him again.

"How I remember those days. He was an ideal lover even then and I will never forget those wonderful days we spent in the park."

This girl came every day and always brought a potted plant. I grew rather to like her, even if her talk and actions were queer. Then a day came when she did not appear. I looked for her each afternoon, but she never came again.

It had been a heavy day at the cemetery and I was ready to go home. I looked at my watch. Only a few more minutes now and I would be free.

A big roadster drew up to the door of the mausoleum. I went to meet the driver who was stepping out, a black clad figure, draped with a heavy veil. Some widow or daughter recently bereaved, I assumed, and ran through the late list in my mind, trying to place the slim young figure, whom I must have seen before.

What was my surprise then, to hear a choking voice ask to be directed to Valentino's tomb.

I led her through the empty corridors and pointed out the crypt.

With an outcry the girl threw herself upon the floor, and sobbed, "I can't go on! I can't! Oh, Rudy! Why did you leave me? Let me come to you!"

I tried to soothe her. I took her a glass of water, endeavored to calm her hysteria. But she resented me, motioned me away, would have nothing to do with me. And her shrieks rang out louder than ever. She lay there for some time on that cold marble floor.

I tried to recall some love affair of Valentino's which might have included this young lady, but I could not. What was the mystery here? I waited until the outburst was over. I wanted to go home!

At last, exhausted, she fell into a sort of faint there on the floor. I could not lock the door and leave the girl here. Finally I decided to do a bit of detective work. I opened her purse and searched until I came to a bit of identification. I recognized her name at once, a name well known in Los Angeles.

Leaving the girl as she was, I went to the telephone and talked with her mother. I told her what had happened. The mother told me she would come at once, which she did. Between us we managed to get the young lady on her feet and out to the car.

I have since watched with interest the social career of this young woman. Very soon after the cemetery episode I read of her leaving for Honolulu. Following that came the announcement of her engagment to a prominent young lawyer of Los Angeles. Now I occasionally see her picture on the society pages with her two children, but never have I seen her at the cemetery since that day six years ago.

CHAPTER VIII

Comments and statements concerning Valentino were, of course, numberless at the time of his death. I quote a few here.

The ones from those who worked with him and knew him best are especially significant.

CHARLES CHAPLIN: "The death of Rudolph Valentino is one of the great tragedies that has occurred in the history of the motion-picture industry. As an actor he achieved fame and distinction; as a friend he commanded love and admiration. We of the film industry, through his death, lose a very dear friend, a man of great charm and kindliness."

VILMA BANKY, who played opposite Valentino to his two pictures, "The Son of the Sheik" and "The Eagle": "Playing opposite Rudolph Valentino taught me the meaning of courtesy and consideration in a fellow actor. He was one of the screen's greatest lovers; he also was one of Hollywood's most perfect gentlemen. I shall mourn him as a friend, but I shall also be happy to remember that I had the opportunity of working opposite him."

GEORGE FITZMAURICE, who directed Valentino: "He was one of the finest gentlemen as well as one of the most finished character actors whom I have ever directed. Rudy knew everybody in his company from the prop man up, and he could call each by name. His consideration and unfailing courtesy won him the respect and admiration of all of us. In his death I have lost a friend."

ALICE TERRY, who played opposite the late star in his first memorable success, "The Four Horsemen of the Apocalypse": "His loss to me is a very keen one personally. He was one of the most wonderful personalities of the screen."

JUNE MATHIS, who selected Valentino for his part in "The Four Horsemen": "My long association with Rudolph Valentino endeared him to me greatly. My heart is too full of sorrow at this time to enable me to speak coherently. I only know that his passing has left a void that nothing can ever fill and that the loss to our industry is too great to estimate at this time."

SIDNEY OLCOTT, director of "Monsieur Beaucaire," halted production on his current film for a brief time in memory of his friend.

MAE MURRAY, opposite whom Valentino worked at Universal in two of the first leads he ever had: "Valentino's great quality was a deep sincerity underlying a great strength of character. Like every genius, he had an infinite capacity for hard work and an earnestness that carried him to the highest peak of his art."

CLARENCE BROWN, a close friend: "Valentino's death is the biggest loss the screen has ever had. Not only was he a great artist, but an influence that worked for good throughout the entire industry; an influence that made all pictures better."

AGNES AYRES, who played opposite Valentino in "The Sheik": "His death is doubly affecting to me because, not only were our careers so closely linked in the struggle for picture success, but he had ever proved himself a loyal friend."

NORMAN KERRY, who financed Valentino in his first attempt to break into motion pictures: "The death of my friend is a great shock; my grief is deep. I had hoped for the best."

ALMA RUBENS, friend of the star: "It is hard to realize that Rudy will never answer the call of the camera again. We never realize our affection for a friend until too late. But I am sure that Rudy's greatness will now reach its peak."

REGINALD DENNY: "The screen has lost not only a great artist, but a real man."

BUSTER KEATON: "Death chose a shining mark when it robbed the world of Rudolph Valentino. He was a real man, the soul of fairness. He was an athlete and a sportsman who played the game aboveboard."

JOHN GILBERT: "The death of Valentino is a terrific loss to the screen. He brought it happiness, beauty and art as perhaps no other has. His loss can never be replaced. There was and can be only one Valentino; a great artist and one of the finest gentlemen it has ever been my privilege to call a friend."

RAMON NOVARRO: "Valentino's death has robbed art of a true son. His work and his personality were inspirations to all who knew him."

MRS. MARGARET TALMADGE, mother of the Talmadge girls: "Millions knew him as a great screen artist but they did not know of the many other things which endeared him to his family, his friends and his co-workers. Some of these qualities were his kindliness, his loyalty to his family and his eagerness to help others."

SAMUEL GOLDWYN, producer: "The death of Rudolph Valentino is a great tragedy. It will be felt wherever he was known. He combined the ability of a great artist with the fine qualities of a gentleman, and in his death the motion-picture industry loses a man who cannot be replaced."

JESSE LASKY: "His death is an irreparable loss to screendom. His passing causes me to mourn the loss of a great artist, a true friend and an admirable man."

CECIL B. DE MILLE, producer and a friend of the dead star: "In Mr. Valentino's death we have lost a great artist. But fortunately we can look on death as progress and not as the finish."

JEANIE McPHERSON: "Personally as well as professionally I always have had the greatest admiration for Mr. Valentino. The entire motion-picture industry grieves over the loss of a true gentleman and an exceptional artist."

COLLEEN MOORE: "A lot of sunshine has gone out of the world with the death of Rudolph Valentino, an artist and a gentleman."

SID GRAUMAN: "The screen has lost a great artist in the death of Rudolph Valentino. Hundreds of his friends in Hollywood are mourning today as are millions of his admirers all over the world. In my career as a showman I found Valentino to be a marvelous box-office attraction because of the distinctive characterizations as the ideal lover that he gave to the silver sheet. He had a wonderful personality and in private life was at all times a perfect gentleman and unaffected by the laurels with which he had been crowned. It will be hard to fill his place on the screen."

REGINALD BARKER, president of the Motion Picture Directors' Association: "The screen will never have another Valentino. He had a distinctiveness all his own, and his loss to the cinema world is an irreparable one. News of his death is a great shock to the industry, and members of the motion-picture directors' association were stunned by the tidings of his passing. The name of Valentino will linger long in the memory of screen fans and members of the film industry, for he was equally popular in private life, as he was in the estimation of the millions who admired his acting."

WILL H. HAYS, "czar" of the industry, telephoned the following statement to his New York office from Indianapolis: "I deeply regret Mr. Valentino's death. He has had a distinguished career and was prepared to do yet greater things. His death is a great loss."

DAVID BELASCO: "I was saddened to learn of Mr. Valentino's death. I admired his acting. I thought he was a great artist. The screen has lost one of its radiant personalities."

GLORIA SWANSON: "He was a real artist, a charming gentleman, a true sportsman and a good friend. Both the motion-picture industry and the public have suffered a great loss."

MAJ. EDWARD BOWES, vice-president of the Metro-Goldwyn Corporation: "He was a hard, honest and sincere worker in his profession, and as I happen to know, personally, a clean-living man. He gave the best that was in him to his work and appreciated fully the responsibility which went with the high esteem in which he was held by the public. He will long be remembered and respected for the high standards which he set in his chosen profession."

JOSEPH M. SCHENCK, chairman of the board of directors of the United Artists Company, and Hiram Abrams, president, speaking for that organization, issued a joint statement: "We are greatly grieved and shocked at the great loss. Everyone hoped for the best, especially since the boy had waged so great a fight against the odds. The loss is a great one to us personally, as he was our friend, and is surely a real blow to the motion-picture industry in which he stood so high."

ADOLPH ZUKOR, head of Famous Players-Lasky: "He threw himself into his parts and tried to live the characters he played. The screen has lost a hard worker, an artist and actor who was always trying to better his work and to please his public. In all my contacts with Valentino I knew him as a gentleman of the best type. He was a credit to his profession."

NOAH BEERY: "One thing I admired in him above all else, and that was his sincere appreciation of home life. He was unfortunate in marriage, it appears, but he had the reputation of preferring the quiet home life of a country gentleman to the glitter of metropolitan existence."

VICTOR FLEMING, director: "I have never directed Rudolph Valentino in a picture, but I have known him. He was possessed of many fine qualities and he had a film following that was amazing."

Comments of the press all over the world were, of course, greatly varied. But for the most part it was genuinely appreciative.

The London Daily Express: "He was a great artist who mastered more than any of his contemporaries the genius that lies in simplicity and restraint."

A writer in the New York World: "Romance is the only thing really worth big headlines, and Rudolph Valentino spelt romance."

Heywood Brown: "Valentino had become that priceless thing – a symbol … It is a long sleep to which he has gone, and very soon the thousands will have another symbol to take his place."

But they have put no other symbol in his place.

CHAPTER IX

There is an elderly man who has come to the mausoleum on and off for the past five years. He is well dressed and impressed me as a successful business man, probably keener and more competent than the average. He has always entered and departed silently. He stands before Rudy's crypt with eyes closed and hands folded behind him.

I never questioned him. Everyone has the right to come and go as he pleases.

One day, I was standing in the entrance when he came out. He stopped and spoke.

"I suppose," he said, "that you wonder why I come here so often. I never saw Valentino while he was alive. All I ever saw of him was on the screen. I know little of his life.

"But about a year ago I had an important business deal come up that puzzled me. I was trying to decide upon the right course to pursue, and seemed to get nowhere near a decision. Suddenly, for no reason that I could see, I remembered that a number of years ago, while Valentino was alive, I handled a transaction for him that brought him a nice profit.

"I am regarded as a hard headed business man and not at all flighty. Yet, I found myself coming here to make my first visit. Several times I started back, telling myself that I must be losing my mind. But I seemed to be drawn on. Well, while I stood there in front of the crypt, that first time, my brain seemed to clear in regard to the deal that had been worrying me. I went home and closed it, with good results.

"Since then, whenever I am puzzled I come here."

I asked him if he was a spiritualist.

"I never have been," he replied. "I have always closed my mind to anything that I felt bordered on superstition. But this thing," he said slowly, "I cannot explain.

"Today I thought I would tell you the reason for my visits, as they may have seemed odd to you."

He asked me not to mention any of this to anyone who might inquire, and went away. He still comes once in a while.

There came one day a dark eyed girl. I think she was an Italian. Her name was Marie, and her home was in New York. She knelt at Rudy's crypt and said a prayer, then kissed the cold marble. She smiled at me through her tears when she saw me near her.

"I have come a long way to be near him," she said. "I saw him in his casket in New York. They had to take me away, for I became hysterical. I wanted to come to California when they brought his body here, but my husband would not let me. I expected that he wouldn't, so I stayed with him for a while.

"But when I had saved a little money, I left New York and headed for Chicago. I hitch-hiked and worked my way. I had a good job in a restaurant in Chicago, but Valentino's spirit kept calling. I continued hitch-hiking until I arrived here. But never again. It is too dangerous. Many are the nights I cried myself to sleep in some auto camp and wished myself back home."

As I left her, she took out her prayer beads and performed her devotions. She stayed until I locked the mausoleum for the night. Each day, after she had looked for work, Marie would come to the cemetery. She always brought flowers and would sit and say her prayers.

One night, after closing time, I happened to return to the mausoleum for something I had forgotten. I found Marie trying to get into the small window near Valentino's crypt. I saw that there was a man with her. I hurried over and asked them what they were doing.

They were frightened, and Marie explained in a faltering voice:

"This is my husband. He has followed me out here to take me home. I didn't want to leave without saying good-bye to Rudy. We are starting back to New York tonight."

I told them to come around to the door and I would let them in. This they did, and I left them alone by Rudy's crypt. After a while I went down to see why they were so long. The husband was trying to drag Marie away, while she cried, "Rudy! Rudy!" At last I told her that she must go, because it was getting late. Still crying Rudy's name, she made her way down the road into the night, a pitiful little figure.

One day as I was working about the building, I heard a car slide to a stop outside the door. I looked up to see three large men step out and come into the mausoleum. In broken English they inquired the direction to the tomb of Valentino, using plenty "dese" and "dems" in their speech. They crowded around the crypt, touching the bronze name plate and feeling of the flowers.

One of them said, "Let us saya de prayer, for da boy."

They got down on their knees. Each one tried to outdo the other, and their prayers rose almost to a shout. When they had finished they arose. One of the fellows, with a shamefaced sort of grin, whispered, "Say, bo, is it alla right to hava one flower, so I cana take it backa to my gal in Chicago?"

I told him as well as the others that they could have a flower if they wished. They were so pleased that they gave me their address and invited me to visit them, should I ever come their way. Then each took a flower and placed it tenderly in tissue paper, which one of the men had drawn from his pocket. After putting the flowers away they asked my name and once again reminded me to look them up. They then bade Rudy a farewell, shook hands with me, and drove away.

It was a rainy day and not a soul had come for hours. The mausoleum was anything but a pleasant place on a day so dark and dreary. I was standing in the doorway watching the rain come down when I heard footsteps splashing up the road. I wondered who would be out on such a day. Presently an old lady came into view. She was wearing a long black coat and a faded shawl wrapped around her head. She was wet to the skin.

She smiled when she saw me and said, "Hell, son! Kinda bad weather, ain't it?"

I answered, "Yes, it is; but it doesn't seem to bother you. You should not come out in this weather. You might get sick."

"Oh I am all right," she answered. "I won't get sick. I just had to come today to see Rudy. He has been with me all the time lately, and I could not get any peace. So I took my umbrella and started off. But when I had gone but a short ways a gust of wind blew my umbrella inside out, so that is why I am so wet."

I had a small heater in the mausoleum, and I invited her to sit near it and get dry. But first she went to pay her respects to Rudy.

"Come," she said. "Please come with me. I am afraid, when it's dark and gloomy."

Together we made our way to Rudy's crypt. She went up and placed her hand on the marble front and whispered, "Rudy, I am here. How are you, dear boy? Please watch over your mother as she is lonesome for you, today and always. I can feel you near me and it gives me courage to go on. I will say a prayer for you tonight when I go to sleep. Good-bye, dear boy!"

"Why do you cry, mother?" I questioned. "What is it that makes you grieve so for him?"

She smiled through her tears as she answered, "Come, we will go sit by the fire and I will tell my story."

After we were seated she said, "You have never seen me before, have you?"

I answered that I had not.

"Well, I have seen you. And do you know that when you are in this building alone there is always one or two of the earthbound spirits watching over you? Many is the time I have seen visions of you in this mausoleum. You are the keeper of the dead and even Rudy watches over you . . . But to come to my story.

"It was years ago when Rudy was a star in pictures and I was doing a bit of extra work. He came up to me one day and said, "Mother, life is so difficult. So many people have different ways of living. I wish I could leave it all and forget I am an actor. I would like to get away from everything and just be myself again.'

He always came to me after that and unburdened his heart. He was heart-broken over his love affairs, and I knew that deep down he still held the love for his first wife, Jean Acker. He told me many of his happiest hours were spent with her.

"One thing I will never forget was when he told me that he wished the men would not hold it against him, because the women made such a fuss over him. He wanted to be happy, but it seemed it was not to be. Now, when he is gone, I live over our little talks we had together.

"He comes to me in my dreams, holding out his arms as if he was groping for something. I think that what he was looking for was love. I awake at night and I can see him looking, always looking with those dark eyes that I had come to love. That's why I come. You have never seen me, because I used to come at night, when I couldn't sleep. I would come and sit by his window and live again the times when we were friends. So, my boy, life is a great lesson. It teaches us to make ourselves better for the sake of mankind. We must get right with ourselves before we go to the other world where Rudy is."

Some visitors then drove up to see Rudy's place. After I had shown them his crypt, I asked if they would be so kind as to take the old lady home. They said they would be glad to and as they drove off she thanked me and said she would come back some other day. This she did but soon after she ceased to visit and I often wonder where she is.

There are a lot of superstitious people who come here. Just the other day a young man came to me and asked where he could find Valentino's tomb. He seemed to have something the matter with him, for he shook, now and then; and his eyes kept roaming all over the place. I told him to go down the corridor as far as he could and then turn right, towards the windows. I called after him, telling him it was easy to find. "Easy!" he exclaimed. "What do you mean?"

Again I explained just where to go.

He pretended not to understand, so I said "Come on. I will show you."

I noticed that he crossed his fingers and followed close at my heels, peering into every corner. I asked him if he was afraid and he replied with a sickly look, "No, not afraid, but places like this give me the willies."

When we came to Valentino's locality, he gave one look, then turned and ran as fast as he could. When I got to the door he was nearly a block down the road.

A colored girl, rather good looking and dressed in nice clothes, came to the mausoleum on a dark January day. The weather did not add to the cheerfulness of the place, by any means. The girl, looking in through the door, held back as if she were afraid to enter. I approached her and asked if I could be of any help.

She inquired, "Is this the tomb of Mr. Rudolph Valentino?"

I told her it was the mausoleum that sheltered the remains of many people, and Valentino was one of them.

"My goodness!" she exclaimed. "Are there lots of dead people inside? Can you see them laying around, or are they all locked up? I don't want to see no corpses!"

I had to laugh and I told her, "Come in and look around. I will show you Valentino's crypt and also some of the other noted ones."

"All right, mister," she said. "Ise coming, but I wants you to stay close to me. It looks mighty dark in that there building, and I don't want to be left alone nohow."

She tiptoed at my heels until we reached the crypt of Valentino. When I pointed it out, she walked up to the bronze name plate and put her hand on it. Her face filled with an awe that was half fear. Turning to me, she said:

"Ise never thought I'd live to see the day Ise could put my hands on a dead man's tomb. But that man was my movie sweetheart, and Ise made myself strong so I could come and see where he was buried among the dead people." She suddenly backed away from the crypt. "Ise had enough of dead people! Ise going out quick and get me some good old fresh air. Thank you, mister. Don't you let them spirits get you!"

She half ran from the building.

One day as I entered the corridor where Valentino is, I saw a boy of about fourteen standing before Rudy's crypt. He was a small framed lad, dressed in a neat suit. His face was a picture of mental anguish when he beheld me near. His eyes were like those of a deer I once wounded when I was a boy, a look I shall always remember.

With a frightened gesture he asked, "Is it all right for me to see Valentino's crypt? Is it all right for me to come in here? I saw no one around to ask, and Rudy's spirit seemed to draw me here."

I answered, "Why, sure it's all right for you to come. Anyone can come, for everyone is welcome. And you can stay as long as you like."

The fear in his eyes faded, and a look of hope appeared.

"Gee," he exclaimed, "that's swell! I sure was afraid when you came in, you looked so big and spooky in your white clothes. You might not believe this," he went on, "but Valentino's spirit has a strange influence over me. I am very psychic, and people from the spirit world bother me. I became so nervous that I could not study in school, and my mind was in a daze. I also play the violin and have to study so hard to make any headway that at last I could stand it no longer. I told my mother I had to give up one or the other. She said to wait a few days and if things did not get better, she would take me on a vacation. Today, while I was on my way to take my music lesson, Valentino's spirit had such a strong influence upon me that it just seemed to draw me here."

Just then a woman who has a daughter interred in the mausoleum came up to me and asked me for a basket. While she spoke, she lifted her hand as if to brush something from her shoulder.

The boy cried out, "Don't do that! There is a girl standing at your back, and she is trying to put her arms around you. She is someone you love, and she is trying to let you know that she is near."

I stood spellbound at his words, and the lady was frightened.

"What do you mean?" she cried. "How can you tell? I see – feel nothing!" She turned and looked behind her.

"Yes," the boy said. "There was a girl there. She is gone now. I think it must be someone you lost – a daughter." He went on to describe how the girl had looked.

The woman was bewildered. "You have described my daughter," she told him, "exactly as she looked. She has been gone for some time now."

"I am psychic," the boy answered, "and I see things other people do not. I shall try and get a message from her; and if I do I shall return and give it to this man. Or, if you will show me where your crypt is, I shall leave it among your flowers. I must go now."

She thanked him and he walked away. We never saw him again.

Of all the people who are loyal to Valentino's memory, there is one who stands out. She is an Italian woman and comes to the mausoleum three or four times a week. Although she had never seen Valentino in real life she had formed such an attachment for him in pictures, that when he died, she and her husband sold their home in San Diego and moved to Los Angeles. They now have a home within walking distance of the cemetery.

A few years after they came here she had a baby which died at birth. She named it after Valentino. The baby's crypt is near that of Valentino, and many people mistake it for his. She brings fresh flowers from her garden. These she divides equally between her baby and Rudy. She also takes care of the flowers brought in by other visitors and fixes these with loving care. Then, with her Bible in hand, she sits for hours reading and saying her prayers. Often I have heard her crying, and it is quite pitiful to hear her weep for her loved ones. Many times after I have closed the mausoleum, she will walk by the windows nearest her crypts and continue to say her prayers.

She claims Valentino has come to her at night and talked with her. In her broken English she says, "Mr. Pete, the spirit of Rudy come to my house. He knocks on walls, sometime on door. I feel him close to me. He say he help me to be happy and he is glad I come to bring flowers to him."

She has met Valentino's brother and sister. On Rudy's birthday and anniversary of his death, she always arranges the flowers so that it is very pretty when they arrive. They have become good friends and she tells me that Alberto has been to her home for a visit.

He was only about four feet tall. With the huge hump and his distorted features, he was a pitiful little specimen of humanity. I felt sorry for him, making his way up the steps to the mausoleum.

He paused as he reached the doorway. I spoke to him and asked him if he would like to see Valentino's resting place.

"Gee!" he cried in amazement. "Do you care if I come in and look around?"

When I assured him that I didn't; that he was welcome to stay as long as he wished, the poor little fellow was almost overcome.

"Gee," he said again reverently as he peered about the spacious corridors. "With all these stained glass windows and everything, it's just like a church in Pittsburgh." He turned to me, "That's where I came from, you know – Pittsburgh. I saw Valentino in all of his pictures there."

We had now reached the crypt, and when the hunchback saw Valentino's name on the bronze plate he knelt on his bony knees and said a prayer. A lump rose in my throat and my heart went out to this misshapen youth as he crouched there on the marble floor.

When he arose, tears were streaming down his cheeks. His voice choked as he said, "I am not like other people. I used to picture myself as Valentino. He meant everything to me. It's kinda tough to be like me, but there probably was some reason for it. I believe there is a great beyond where we go when we finish this life, and I hope to get a break there."

He asked if I minded if he stayed a while. Of course I told him that I didn't and went and got a chair for him.

Nearly three hours later, when I returned, I found the poor chap curled up in the chair, fast asleep. He told me:

"I fell asleep here and dreamed that Rudy came up to me and told me he was glad I had come to visit his tomb. Then he faded right away again." The hunchback gave a quick glance about him. "Say," he continued, "He- Rudy, I mean – he couldn't get out of there, could he?" He pointed at the crypt.

I smiled and said I didn't think that possible. The little fellow looked immensely relieved. He asked me if he might have a flower from the bouquet on the crypt. I told him that he could pick it out himself. That pleased him greatly. I also gave him a few beads from the wreath.

His eyes misted again as he thanked me. "No one has ever treated me so kindly before. Why are you so good to me?"

I answered him, "Just because you are an unfortunate is no reason for people around you to be unkind. Whenever you are around stop in here if you care to."

I never saw him again. Poor soul, I hope he is all right, and that he gets his break when he finishes this cycle of life.

I will always remember Jean Acker as one of the sweetest girls I have ever met. She came to the mausoleum with a girl friend, each carrying a large bouquet of flowers for Rudy.

I did not know it was Jean until after we had the flowers arranged. She asked me many questions about the people who came to visit Valentino. I was curious as to who she was. I soon got my opportunity when Jean knelt to say a prayer. The other girl and I walked away so she could be alone. On my inquiry as to who she was, the friend said, "That is Jean Acker, Valentino's first wife. When she is through I will introduce you to her." This she did and after that Jean and I became very good friends.

Whenever she comes to Hollywood she pays Rudy a visit. When she is away she telegraphs orders for flowers. These are sent to the mausoleum, where I arrange them.

She was with Rudy when he died. When I asked her about it, she said, "It was so unreal to see Rudy lying in bed dying. To me it seemed like a publicity stunt. I got the priest to administer the last rites of the church, when I found out there was no hope. I thank God I was there when Rudy went away. He was more than a friend, he was part of my life."

I made it possible for Jean to talk with Alberto a short time later. When I saw her again, she said, "When Alberto talked to me over the phone, I thought it was Rudy. His voice sounded exactly like his and for a moment I was speechless."

Jean has been very kind to me and I value her friendship.

CHAPTER X

The Mysterious Veiled Lady in Black

The eleventh anniversary of Valentino's death has passed. Others will follow, but if they reveal a fraction of the loyalty and devotion which marked this one, in numbers of visitors and in gorgeous display of floral offerings to Rudy's memory, I will know that the man will never be forgotten.

Over a thousand admirers, on August 23, 1937, paid homage to the departed star. There was the regular basket of flowers given by the Valentino Association in London, and that from the Valentino Memorial Club of Chicago. Miss Fanny Lichtenfeld of Richmond, Virginia and Miss Emma Leutgeb of Salzburg, Austria, paid tribute by sending money for red roses to be placed at the actor's tomb. These and many other men and women have been faithful to every anniversary for years.

Newspapermen and cameramen from the Press Associations and from many of the major newspapers in the country were at hand to write and take pictures of the event. These came early. They were at the mausoleum when I opened the doors on the morning of August 23.

I was a little surprised and I must have showed it in my face, for presently one of the newspaper men remarked: "I suppose you wonder why we're here so early." Before I could answer he continued: "We want to get the low-down on this mysterious lady in black who comes to see Valentino. When do you expect her?"

They crowded around me, their faces eager as they waited for an answer. I had to suppress a grin. They were certainly on the hunt for the little woman, that mysterious lady in black.

Who is she, this elusive veiled lady, who comes to Valentino's tomb? Thousands of Valentino's admirers want to know. Where is she from, they ask. What does she look like? Why does she do it? Is she one of Rudy's wives? Is she Pola Negri?

The world wants to know and these men are here on the chance that she may put in an appearance. They have hopes that she will come. The public demands an answer and they will not fail – if they can only find her! But so far, they have been unable to recognize her. They have begun to believe that she comes and goes like a phantom, and that is not far from the truth.

However, I am a little ahead of my story. I will go back to the time I first met this charming lady.

It was several years ago. How well I remember that January day. I had been standing on the mausoleum steps gazing at the mountains which rose majestically above the foothills towards the north-east. Their jagged peaks had been newly crowned with a mantle of snow the night before, and they were dazzling under the bright sun.

So absorbed was I in the spectacle that I was unaware that someone had approached me. A soft voice jarred me from my thoughts.

"Please sir, can you direct me to Valentino's tomb?"

I turned quickly and saw a heavily veiled woman of medium height standing within a few feet of me. How she had been able to approach so silently, without my hearing her, I could not understand.

A low laugh came from behind the heavy folds of the veil as she read my amazement. "I'm so sorry," she apologized. "I didn't mean to startle you."

By this time I had recovered my composure. I could make nothing of her face through the black cloth. In fact, all I could make out was the gentle contour of her face. (I was puzzled to know how she could see through it herself.) I smiled at her and told her that it was quite all right, but that if she would whistle the next time I'd be prepared.

Together we walked into the mausoleum. She said very little, and when we reached Rudy's crypt I left her and returned to the main corridor.

In fifteen minutes I went back to see if I could be of any service to her, but found her gone. This surprised me, for I was positive that she had not passed me in the main corridor, which leads to the one and only entrance to the building.

I explored the other smaller corridors, sure that I would find her in one of them, but the search was fruitless. She was nowhere in the building. I thought of her often, for I was much puzzled at her strange disappearance.

The next time I saw her was about two weeks later. I was showing some visitors through the mausoleum and, when we entered Valentino's corridor, there she was. She was standing in front of Rudy's crypt with hands pressed on the marble front, and looking intently at the name plate. She wore the same heavy veil. When she heard us approach, the cloth made a little swish of sound as she turned her head to see who was coming.

I said "Hello" to her and she answered in her soft voice. Then with a graceful movement she swept by us and hurried away.

Of course the people with me were curious and questioned me concerning her. but I could not answer them, for she still was a stranger to me.

I met her many times after that, but it was always under similar circumstances. It seemed that the only time I would come upon her was when I least expected to see her. How she ever managed to move about so silently I don't know. I never questioned her about this, however, and let her come and go without molestation.

She was a very neat person, and her clothes, though invariably black, were always of the best of taste. So far as I could guess she was a woman of about thirty.

She took to bringing flowers on her visits, and usually they were red roses, Valentino's favorite. Many times after an absence from the mausoleum, I would find upon my return, red roses in Rudy's vases, and I knew that she had paid him a visit.

Rumors of this mysterious woman spread, and some people laid in wait for her. A few times she was seen by these curious ones, and she had some difficulty getting away from them. I rescued her on these occasions and she seemed grateful.

I told her that perhaps it would be better if she came unveiled, then she wouldn't attract so much attention. I explained that many people came to pay homage at Valentino's tomb and that, if she came wearing nothing which would distinguish her from others, no one would notice her.

At first she seemed reluctant to do this, but after I assured her that I wouldn't tell who she was she said she would try it out.

That was a memorable day for me when I got my first look at her face. She burst into a laugh as I stood and stared at her. She was beautiful, with a marvelous skin, and her makeup was just right. But what I liked best of all was her eyes. They were deep and clear. Long eyelashes shaded them.

I told her it certainly was a treat to look at her and see her as she really was. We chatted for sometime. As I walked with her down the corridor to Rudy's crypt she told me that she was going away, but that she would return in a few months.

After paying her respects to Valentino she said good-bye to me and went her way. She returned again sometime after that and then disappeared again.

She always managed to come on the anniversary August 23, and on his birthday May 6th. She wore her veil on several of these occasions and, as she offered no explanation, I never asked her for any.

So that is the story of the mysterious veiled lady in black. I explained to the newspaper men that she had already paid a visit on August 20, which was Friday, a few days before the anniversary.

Did I think she would be here today, they wanted to know.

I told them that there was a good chance of her coming, but not to be disappointed if she failed to appear. I told them that she would be sure to know that someone would be here to snap her picture and ask her questions, for yesterday's papers had had articles about her.

"Well, we're going to stay all day if necessary," they said. "And we'll sure get her if she does arrive."

And all day they did stay. They got a few pictures of other women who came, but not one of the mysterious lady.

She was here in the cemetery, all right, but she did not approach the mausoleum. I saw her sitting down by the lake on a marble bench and when I could make it possible I went down and talked with her. She was disturbed at first, when I approached, but I told her I would not tell that she was here.

She told me that she was going away again for awhile and that she would like to go inside and pay tribute to Rudy's memory. She asked if there was any possible way for her to enter the mausoleum without danger of being recognized.

I told her there was none. She was deeply disappointed. Then a thought struck me. I told her that if she would wait, I would leave as usual at closing time, then come back and let her in.

This she consented to do.

At five o'clock I locked up the mausoleum, and the newspaper men and I left the cemetery at the same time. I circled a few blocks, then returned. Sure enough, she was there waiting for me. She had a small bouquet of roses and I let her in. I did not follow her and she came out in a few minutes.

I offered her a ride to wherever she would like me to take her. She said that if I would drive her to the car line that would be far enough. This I did, and that is the last I have seen of her up to this writing.

The papers came out with stories that the mystery woman had failed to put in an appearance at Rudy's crypt. I had to smile when I read that.

Unforgotten
Pictures of
Rudolph Valentino

Rudolph Valentino – portrait taken by his favorite photographer Mabel Sykes in Chicago

Rudolph Valentino – portrait taken by Shirley Blane in Los Angeles

Rudolph Valentino posing in character as a pirate

Rudolph Valentino portrait taken around 1924

Rudolph Valentino portrait taken in his Whitley Heights home, 1923

Rudolph Valentino posing in a bathing suit while smoking. Very casual indeed!

Rudolph Valentino photographed standing at the bow of his yacht The Phoenix, circa late 1925

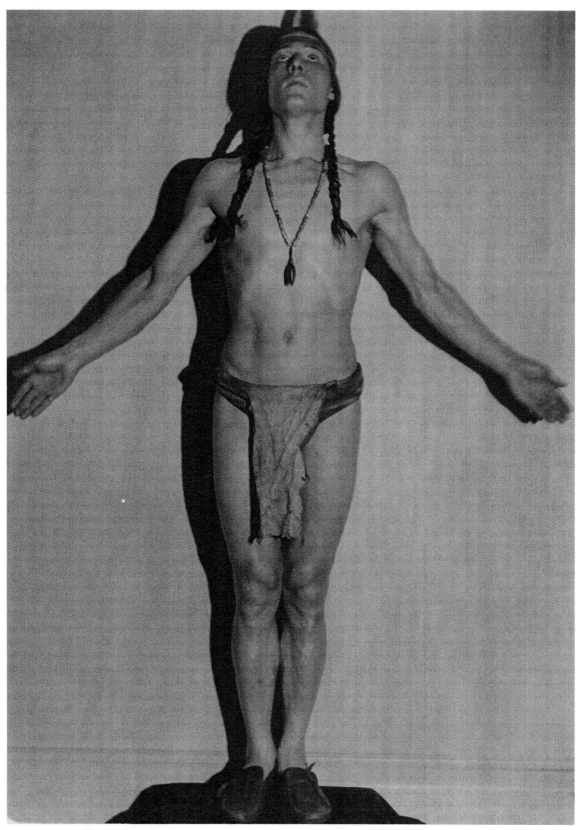

Rudolph Valentino poses as an American Indian in this 1922 photograph

Rudolph Valentino in *The Four Horseman of the Apocalypse*, dated 1921. With his touching portrayal of Julio Desnoyers Valentino obtained stardom.

Rudolph Valentino in one of his rare pre-star films where he didn't play the scoundrel. Here is a scene from Universal Pictures 1918 film *All Night*. Valentino's character was named Richard Thayer

Rudolph Valentino as Amos Judd in a portrait photo from the
1922 Paramount Pictures film *The Young Rajah*

CHAPTER XI

The widespread interest in every possible analysis of the character of Valentino has brought about numerous studies of his handwriting, his astrological horoscope, his name in connection with numerology. For the benefit for those who are interested in these subjects, A. Henry Silver, well known graphologist, has been kind enough to furnish the author with the following.

GRAPHOLOGICAL ANALYSIS OF RUDOLPH VALENTINO

From specimen of his handwriting of Feb. 14, 1926

The interpretations of Rudolph Valentino's characteristics through the medium of graphology, the science of reading character from handwriting, are based upon an exact science in that the mental and physical characteristics are revealed solely by the muscular nervous actions, controlled by the nervous system, which in turn is controlled by the mental and physical impressions registered on the nervous system at the time of writing. The law governing the interpretation is a basic and natural one, that of "the law of relation." The following analysis is based upon handwriting specimens executed by Valentino Feb. 14, 1926:

Moods, emotions, tastes and temperaments are the surface characteristics and some people are very inconsistent in their display of them. But with Valentino we will find he was exceptionally consistent, undoubtedly a strong factor responsible for the height of his success.

Valentino had developed his writing so that it kept on an even keel, revealing he had trained himself to a practical sense of realities. The fact that he would subconsciously boost up the base of each following word to keep the line of writing from going down hill proves that he had developed, through force of will, the habit of not permitting his mood from being despondent or pessimistic. Whenever he felt himself slipping he consistently snapped out of it. This unusual action in his handwriting reveals that in his younger days he must have been more or less moody but through sheer force of will cured himself of it.

There was no artificial or suppressed emotion with Valentino. His consistent forty-five degree angle of slant in writing reveals he was natural and free in his emotional display.

His medium-size writing showed his good judgment and sense of proportion and that he had no basic inclination toward either pettiness or "four-flushing."

The consistency of placing his "t-bars" deliberately on the "t-stems" reveals he was deliberate in thought and action resulting in efficiency, and the frequent little knots on the left end of the "t-bar" showed he usually weighted facts before acting and could seldom be rushed into a decision.

The medium weight pressure on the "t-bar," also consistent with Valentino, reveals he displayed a happy medium in the exertion of his will. There was no lack of will force, neither did he desire to "boss" or rule others, but was amenable to reason and had respect for others' rights.

His connecting links of letters were consistently firm and exceptionally interesting – in that the action of the hand is subconscious while writing. Valentino's letter connections were executed methodically even. This action not only shows he had the ability of protecting his interests, but coupled with the aforesaid characteristics and others mentioned in the following, reveals he possessed a high degree of courage, much above the average. Regardless of his firmness, however, he did not possess any habitual characteristics of bad temper or quarrelsomeness, as his handwriting is wholly void of any sharp or angular connections of his letters.

Also his handwriting lacks the characteristic that reveals conceit or crampness of writing that would show stinginess. He had none of this. And while he was generous he was not extravagant, for his curtailed final strokes at the end of words reveals that he had a good sense of thrift and of values.

Strange as it may seem, with one who became known so spectacularly to millions, Valentino had no undue craving for the limelight or spectacularism, for his capital letters reveal no extreme spectacular actions.

The characteristics in handwriting controlled by intellect are basic and the surface characteristics or habits are influenced by one's intellect.

Valentino's writing reveals one who natively had a very high intellect.

His exceptionally even base-line within the words and the even height letters show he was consistently dependable and possessed a very high sense of honor and integrity. For this reason he could easily view others with trust, as possessing these same high qualities. Also, deep down, he was not proud but quite democratic as revealed by his moderate height capital letters.

His sharp-pointed "n's" and "m's" prove he possessed a keen wit and a great sense of humor. The closing of most of his "a's" and "o's" reveal he would talk freely with people he trusted. While there are no actions in his writing revealing any habit of stubbornness, nevertheless he had plenty of fighting instinct and would carry through to a strong finish if he thought he was right. This characteristic is disclosed by the positive down-ending stroke of his "g's" and "y's" at the ends of words.

One of the most interesting actions in Valentino's handwriting, the many disconnections of the letters within the words, reveal he was highly intuitive or psychic. He would have been very adept in delving into the occult. This ability of mind is what is called "genius," but a quality which causes its possessor to be, on occasions, much misunderstood by others. Such a mind would of course be very sensitive, not only to influences from within, but to influences from without.

Valentino, being extremely intuitive, may often have appeared illogical to others possessing mere logical type of minds, when he was following his subconscious promptings. However, the chances are that if these same people had followed his advice, those concerned would have been better off.

Certain types of roles he was forced to portray during his dramatic career undoubtedly caused millions to gain a misunderstanding of the true nature of the man. This resulted possibly in many unfair criticisms being directed his way – a condition which would cause him much mental suffering. Valentino, having a very sensitive mind and being one who valued the truth, would therefore have deeply desired these same millions to know him for what he really was – a man of courage, honor and integrity. It is safe to say that no one knew Valentino as well as he knew himself and any unfair criticism of his character would hurt him very much. His sensitive nature responding to such conditions undoubtedly was responsible for developing his one great weakness – this is shown by many of the endings of his words curling upward and back—an action in his writing revealing almost fanatical self-consciousness. In his particular case psychological reasons would make it quite safe to say this action did not appear in his handwriting in his younger day, but was unconsciously developed later from certain happenings brought about through force of circumstances during his film career.

These happenings caused his high sense of spirituality and idealism to subconsciously invert within himself, resulting in an extreme consciously governed self-watchfulness – a habit of watching his every action so that others might have a true conception of his character. But only Valentino, himself, bore all the hurts and sufferings resulting from this later characteristic developed from his extreme sensitiveness.

Valentino, possessing such a strong combination of consistent characteristics as revealed already in this analysis, would have been successful in any vocation he had chosen to follow. However, his handwriting reveals he was naturally adapted to art.

The squareness or block formation of his writing shows a fine sense of balance and of mathematics and he could have been a very successful architect or construction engineer. His methodically and evenly spaced letters reveal a wonderful sense of rhythm and taste for accuracy and neatness, making him highly efficient in dancing. He loved music with good rhythm and music lacking it would soon tire him. He also had a very deep appreciation toward beauty of form – revealed by the artistic form of his capital letters. The high upper-stroke of his small letter "p" reveals a skillful mind and skillful fingers and he would have been highly efficient in handling anything such as the paint brush, pen, pencil, sculpturing knife or surgical instruments.

The consistently even pressure in Valentino's handwriting reveals that he possessed much physical strength. The steady lines of the writing and steady baseline of the words reveal steady nerves. The long slender loops of the "g's" and "y's" show he possessed not only strong limbs but limbs that could be skillfully manipulated.

In his specimen of writing executed in February, 1926, he shows one outstanding impediment, caused from a physical condition revealed especially in the "a's" and "o's". Valentino had difficulty in making these letters without causing unnatural breaks and the breaks were more pronounced on the left side of the letters. This action is repeated in the same position in the "a's" and "o's" and similar movements through-out the writing, which proves they were not a slip of the pen. Such an action reveals at that period of time Valentino suffered from an abdominal impediment, more pronounced on the left side. A physical impediment is thrown into the lines of writing in relation to the position of the impediment in the body, a reaction controlled by the natural "law of relation," the basic principal governing the interpretation of a person's characteristics from handwriting.

CHAPTER XII

Numerology, according to those whom I have consulted on the subject, is a science that explains every expression of life and character. It is, to quote from David Strong, who is an exponent, "the practical application of the fundamental laws of mathematics to the natural existence of man – the definition and exact meaning of each number in its relation to life."

Dr. Juno Kayy Walton, in constructing the following analysis, merely makes notes of the name of the man and then worked out this "numberscope." It is based solely upon the analysis of the name, as the chart shows.

I am very grateful to Dr. Walton for this work. If the name of the subject had been Jim Smith instead of Rudolpho Alfonzo Raffaelo Pierre Filibert Guglielmi Valentina d'Antonguella I am inclined to believe that the task might have been somewhat simpler.

NUMBERSCOPE OF RUDOLPH VALENTINO

BIRTH RECORD

The tragedy which took Rudolph Valentino so suddenly from our midst, threatened from birth. From the first, his birth record suggested this possibility, for it sums up in figures to the strange and karmic number (16) (7), foretelling a deep soul experience and a debt to pay to life.

The debt was not of this lifetime for the numbers of the birth record represent the law of fate in every life and when the number (16) (7) is found here, it tells of a higher law transgressed during a previous life which the soul must adjust and pay for through tribulation, sorrow and loss during this present incarnation. The number embodies an occult and spiritual force, so in fancy we follow his life back to some other world, some distant star and wonder if our lovable, but strangely fascinating Rudolph Valentino may have been a mystic in some temple of high learning who, tempted by romance, love and beauty, broke a sacred vow and was forced to pay in this life by giving his very soul to the world, and to no lasting happiness for himself.

This same number gave him a thoughtful, analytical, intuitive mind, a keen sense of perfection and constantly urged him on to finer expression of his talents, to a higher goal; until he could never be fully satisfied with his performance, dreaming of the time when he would reach perfection in his art, touched by a divine power for he must have been subjectively aware of this greater power which he knew in other times and other lives.

His birth number shows him to be of a reserved nature, sensitive and retiring. He had a love of solitude and could only be at his best through periods of aloneness and meditation, which may have made him seem exclusive, difficult and hard to understand at times, even to those who loved him most; and there were undoubtedly times in his association with others when he seemed cold, separate and unloving, for this mystical tendency placed a barrier between him and ordinary human understanding. He could not always reveal his innermost thought for he felt a lack of understanding in others of this complex nature and knew that his desires and longing were foreign and unknowable even to those who longed to be a part of his every thought.

He could be critical and extremely exacting, demanding explanations of others which he did not give himself; sometimes a little sarcastic in speech when displeased or annoyed, showing a manner of superiority. But these were only human traits and did not really mar the beauty of his character, for he idealized all that was in love and friendship. He could be childlike in his response to love, approval and admiration. This helped to balance the odd, strange and peculiar which was the divine side of his nature.

CHARACTERISTICS

That one's name is indicative of character and talent is shown in a convincing manner through Rudolph Valentino's name, for the most striking feature in the Numberscope is the repeated appearance of the number six (6) or number of the artist.

There are ten sixes in the construction of his name and this an unusual occurrence. His name is a long one, it is true, but even so, the indication is far above the normal, for in a name of average length, from (17) to (20) letters, there are seldom more than one or two sixes. There are (69) letters in his name which also digits to six; the number of his heart's desire is (51) or (6) and he was born on the sixth of the month. Every thought and desire of his life was colored by the artistic urge and his temperament was that of the artist. He was born to find a place in the world of art and to bring art to the world for he was so endowed with the quality of artistic feeling that he could not help but inspire this feeling in others.

The number six is not only an artistic influence; it is a humanitarian number and stands for race service and for ideals of the highest order. It is the number of love, sympathy and sacrifice, and there was much of this in his nature. He felt the need of humanity for love, beauty and sympathy and responded to this in his work and interpretation of human emotion. There was a strong sense of justice in his make-up and he suffered through wrongs of injustice and was quick to fight for what he thought was right and he had many deeply ingrained principles of right and wrong. He could be hurt personally, more through lack of truth or justice or loyalty in his friends than by any other thing, and this feeling of loyalty was so strong he could be unreasonable and even unforgiving and hard upon the wrong-doer. But at the same time he could be easily influenced by those who knew how to appeal to this sympathy and sense of loyalty and must have been imposed upon by others, even when he knew better.

He loved a home, the warmth of companionship and had high ideals in love. This is shown by the number of his inner nature or heart's desire. He held the love of the opposite sex very high and was inclined to idealize those he loved and then to suffer when he found them to be just human. He tried to place them on a pedestal of perfection which they could not reach and still be the sweetly human person he also desired for companionship. His ideals became a challenge to him and a love challenge would have followed him all his life because the many sixes colored his dream of companionship. Here, as in his art, he would always struggle for an ideal almost too perfect to be realized.

While he dreamed of the perfect love, he was only human himself for he had firm likes and dislikes. There was a touch of stubbornness hard to meet and he was capable of moods, blunt speech and criticism, for, convinced against his will, he was of the same opinion still. He really needed home, wife, children to balance his life for without sympathetic association he could not be really happy, but because of the karmic debt he had to pay he had to sacrifice these and became instead the never-to-be-forgotten lover of the silver-screen.

TYPE

A long name is sometimes a handicap for it gives much responsibility and much to take care of during a lifetime. It signifies unfinished tasks brought over from previous lifetimes. A short name indicates many problems worked out, fewer burdens to meet. A long name also means many tools and gives an intensity of feeling and thought not found in the name of average length. Rudolph Valentino felt his experiences a thousand times more deeply than other people for there were (12) numbers of expression and imagination in his name, (12) intuitive members of impressionability as well as the ten sixes. Where you or I might feel an emotion, he felt it to a depth beyond our understanding and in those moments when he responded to his intuition, he could sense and feel the hidden and universal laws of being and almost enter the realms of the unseen. He had a practical side to his nature but he was the emotional and intuitive type and did not remain long at the commonplace level of work or thought.

He was not a mental man. He had a fine mind and a brilliant one, but he was not the reasoning or logical thinker. He could not stop to reason things out from the logical point of view for this would only hold him down and limit him. But the many sevens in his name, which is another unusual feature, gave him an analytical type of thought and he often came nearer the truth of things and into a finer relationship of fact than some of the so-called thinking minds. He had skill, technique, and observation, and this gave him finesse and discrimination and ability to know the difference between the real and the unreal. Later in life, had he lived, he would have placed some of his thoughts in books, plays or writings.

But with all his fine talent and clever mentality, he lacked the power of self-direction. Often he could not say definitely "yes" or "no" and really needed a director of strong character, for he was a man of many moods, and many letters in his name could not but make him temperamental and an extremist. He was lucky to have had friends who helped him, for when he came into the outer world of activity he was liable to be buffeted about, without the guiding hand of some sympathetic and understanding advisor. He was too sensitive to be a man of business. Business had to be taken care of by others for real financial success.

His name shows that he was not a worldly man. The number five, the number of the common pleasures of the world appears (12) times in his name, but it is often found from five to six times in an average name. He liked the world, thrilled to the public, but he was not in his right place at a jazz party. He could not help but be confused or side-tracked from the real issues of life through this activity and only needed to touch this from time to time to keep him in touch with the world. He was in the world but not of it, and needed to give his time to dreams, study and the deeper facts of being. Travel, change and excitement were good for him at times, but he needed more; the garden, flowers and the soul of things and to enter too deeply into the gaiety of the world of restaurants, drinking or nightlife was to risk a fall from grace and a loss of his finer powers of attraction. He had nine divisions to his name, also, showing that he lived more truly in the consciousness of the universal and could not live long at the level of the ordinary people. He had to draw others unto him. He could not descent.

CHALLENGE

Every character has a challenge of some sort to meet. Rudolph Valentino had the cipher challenge. This is the greatest challenge a soul can meet. It means naught or all and he came into the world to prove himself, to be naught or all according to his own efforts. This did not make life easy for him and with all his talents he had to make the struggle to gain his ambition and to round out his life. There were times when he, no doubt, thought the struggle was too hard, the goal beyond his strength, and he wondered why he had such a debt to pay, while in other ways he seemed to have all that the world called good. He could have failed many times, for after all the cipher challenge does not help the individual unless the great effort is made. He must have met his challenge, for he filled the heart of the world with love, beauty and grace.

PINNACLES (Periods of Activity)

The master vibration (11) colored his pathway for the first part of his life. From birth until his 31st year he was supported and helped by a spiritual force and influence, even though his challenge demanded his best effort at all times. It was this finer influence which was felt so keenly in his work and which helped him touch the inner lives of so many. It made him very sensitive and was not good for health and gave him an inner nervousness which he often had to control deliberately. He was touched with something of the esthetic and endowed with charm, refinement and personality, and was able to influence others through pleasing manner. His personality, also the number (38) or (11) or (2) helped bring out this spiritual force, graciousness and pleasing personality, and made him one who had many admiring friends and able to influence them or to get them to do anything he wanted them to do. This number helped give him talent for the number (2) is often found in the names of those who dance, or express art through the rhythm of time and music. He had a keen appreciation of music, and it is possible that he might have composed music or developed a pleasing voice had he lived until the day of the talking movie.

This spiritual force shed upon him from his pinnacle helped to make it impossible for him to mix with the common people or to live at the lesser level of living. It also gave him a possibility of trouble in partnerships and associations. He had the desire to associate peacefully with others, to share and cooperate, but he was too much of an idealist to really cooperate fully, even though he tried to do so. There was a bull-dog tenacity and silent determination so strong in his nature that once his mind was made up he was untouched by the advice of others and blind to any other issue. Had he truly learned a little more of cooperation he might have had more peace in his daily associations both in love and business. But, after all, his birth record finds him standing alone in the world, and he could only do that which his inner nature directed him to do, for his greatest success depended upon this higher guidance.

EXPERIENCES

Every letter of a name gives a stated and definite period of experience. His long name intensified his experiences and opened up a gamut of activity and events which is not taken by one having a shorter name. A period of popularity began about the age of (22) and lasted throughout his life. At this time his intuitive nature was awakened and he began to have the power to express his feelings and artistic impressions. This is shown by the "r" and the four times the letter "i" is repeated in the table of events. At about the age of (23) he experienced a turn of events in a new direction with more power or recognition. A chance for important publicity or fame is shown around the age of (25).

At about the age of (22), at the same time he began to develop his talents, the peculiar and mystic influence of the letter "z" entered his affairs. This letter brings a challenge in love affairs and marriage and stood in his way up to the age of (29). It gives influence, position and power to direct the affairs for recognition and honor, but it brings strange conditions into the marriage, unusual happenings or the possibility of a wrong marriage. Even though he loved deeply and idealized love, he was bound to find obstacles in the way of happiness in marriage.

At about the age of (24), a financial influence began to be realized through the letter "g", giving business enterprise and the chance to make money, but at the age of (26) when all was going fine, the karmic influence suggested by the (16) of his birth force began to operate through the letter "p" which is the sixteenth letter of the alphabet, and this forced him to look at life in a more serious manner than he might have done otherwise, considering his success and honor. This letter gives skill, technic and ability to do things well and add a fine mental stimulus towards study, the occult and mysterious. But it tries to keep one in the background and often prevents public influence. In the end of its period of influence, which is seven years, it takes away something; money, honor, love or health. So along with the success he was making, he was also struggling with an emotional problem and barriers between himself and his desires. This letter is often treacherous in its influence and its final effect, and few ever pass through it without loss of something precious, so as it had only one more year to run in his life it may have had something to do with his sudden passing out. It is even possible that he might have experienced a dimming of his popularity in another year or so and perhaps it is well that he passed out before the full effect of this negative force came into operation.

The letter "z" was completed at the age of (29) and a new duty appeared, but of easier and happier nature, giving him more opportunity for love and happiness except for the strange chilling force of the letter "p". There was a love experience between the (28) and (29), something sweet, spiritual and lovely, but whether he gave this thought or not, only his close friends can know for it is hidden deep in his chart of experience. Or he may have hidden it deeply, fearing the difficulties or barriers which had formerly stood in his way. A practical matter due to property and possessions, work and also family held him down between the ages of (27) and (30) and it is possible that during this time those who helped him or directed his affairs compelled him to concentrate his attention to practical matters for his own good. But health conditions also became a problem and should not have been neglected.

LAST YEAR OF HIS LIFE

In 1926 he stood upon the mountain-top of attainment, alone in his position but at a place of transition and making ready for a new effort. The spiritual force of his pinnacle number combined with the spiritual force of the (2) of his personal year. This brought agreements, contracts into the foreground and indicated a change in associations and relationship. During the spring and summer, association or agreement was completed and in the fall a new one was to have been made, for better practical conditions and a firmer foundation. That a better organization of his affairs was needed was shown by the number four summing up his year's experience, and he was in his (31st) year of life also signifying the need of order, system, application and reconstruction.

The very best of his nature was demanded of him on all planes of being, but he passed out on August 23, 1926, a vibration which sums up to a (2) also a four, representing spiritual mastership, and he answered the call to a higher association and left earthly associations behind, going onward to his reward. The message of the Master again re-echoes from the tomb of Rudolph Valentino – "In the world ye have tribulations, but be of good cheer I have overcome the world."

America, the country which loved him dearly has at heart the number (16). Here he met his karma. California has at heart the number of his destiny – (8). Here he found recognition and power for he was destined from birth for authority and power and he will not be quickly forgotten for his destiny number (53) 8 is the number of REGENERATION and the balance between spirit and matter, life and death.   Dr. Juno Kayy Walton

CHAPTER XIII

I am indebted to Paul Foster Case, writer and lecturer, for this third summary of the character of Valentino.

He was asked to give an astrological analysis of a man born in Castellaneta, Italy, at 3 o'clock in the morning of May 6, 1895. He was given the latitude and longitude, but the name of Rudolph Valentino was not mentioned.

Dr. Case dictated the following, conversationally, but from accurate notes. He began, "This person comes under the aspects of the earthly sign of Taurus, the second sign of the zodiac, ruled by Venus.

"What about the personality, the character and the temperament of this man? According to these days and dates he must have had an exceedingly positive personality. He must have been magnetic. He must have been thoughtful and, above all things, he must have been moody but superficially cheerful and jovial. He must have kept himself physically attractive."

Case said that a man born under this sign would be inclined to be very fond of the good things of life. He would be stubborn, would probably be self-willed and possessed of great independence of nature. Such a character would have to apply every effort toward overcoming the emotional and sensitive inclination toward what we may call introversion. It was only through his own efforts that he became what is the greatest combination, an intro-extrovert. That accounts to a very great degree for his success. He was always thoughtful. He was always reflective. He was always a reasoning person. Case, having been informed of the date of birth, the hour of birth, and the place of birth, said: "That man would have a very vivid imagination. That kind of man probably would be a trifle slow in learning some things but once he did learn them they would remain with him forever."

He also said that from his analysis this character should be possessed of a very good physical condition; that he should be very sensitive, and that he should be particularly sensitive in the region of the throat where colds and infections have a tendency to lodge. He said that there would also be an urge or inspiration in such a person to accomplish, to learn, to achieve.

Case further stated: "There would be a strong quality of affection and an equally strong desire for affection, for real companionship and genuine understanding on the part of friends, which would be warmly reciprocated. Passionate, full human sympathy, affectionate, there would be a desire for real love. A desire for harmony and a dislike for unnecessary conflict and friction. Once a friend or a party to a love affair or marriage, there would be a permanent love and loyalty, yet in case of any estranging break there would be no desire to show or express it.

"He, assuming that we are speaking of one of the masculine gender, would be fond of pleasure and filled with an eager love of life. He would be inclined toward sports, entertainment, such physical activities as hunting, motoring, games. He would like to travel. It would be important, too, that his selection of the right kind of wife were careful and well advised. Otherwise a break would be likely to come. A wife who afforded inspiration and help would add much to his success; one lacking real understanding, sympathy and complete love would do much to interfere with happiness and success. He would exert every effort to create happiness for a wife, relations and friends. "While types indicative of his own sign and Scorpio would be likely to appeal to his emotional nature, he would be to a great extent attracted by types indicated by the signs of Cancer, Virgo, Capricorn and Pisces. If one born under the sign of Taurus were to seek advise from an astrologist he would be told the following, in essence: "Keep yourself personally attractive in your domestic life and endeavor to be the same charming personality after marriage that you were before and you will experience greater happiness. Life on earth was intended to be enjoyed, to be lived happily and in harmony, one with another. We can make it so if we will endeavor earnestly to overcome personal selfishness. Use good judgment and foresight in marriage and use its influence for inspiration to rise to heights of success and happiness.

"Know yourself and you will encounter little difficulty in choosing the right type of mate. You will have love, harmony and perhaps children in your home. Realize that children reflect and are the sum total of all that the parents are. Possessing intense love for children, you will be a tender and affectionate parent. "You are fond of quiet and harmonious home atmosphere. As you are somewhat firm and determined in nature you desire, in a sense, to be master in your home; you wish to be free and independent in your domestic life. When this is not forthcoming you are inclined to be moody and irritable. In home surroundings you have a longing for the best money can buy. Conditions permitting, you would decorate your home artistically and appreciate lovely gardens or external surroundings. You are sociable and enjoy entertaining at home with friends and associates to enjoy your hospitality.

"The men of this sign are inclined toward banking, financial matters, salesmen, professors, agriculturists, and it is noted many are good mechanics. The military, legal and medical professions are chosen by members of this sign. The artistic qualities of your nature should receive attention and cultivation regardless of your chosen vocation. People of your sign are also found among the stars of stage and screen while others follow artistic and literary pursuits. Musical talents are also indicated and should be cultivated.

"Your power of will and determination is an asset to you in your efforts to attain success and recognition. Regarding partnerships, good judgment must be used as you are somewhat independent and inclined to have your own way of accomplishing things. You will get along well unless needlessly imposed upon.

"The indications show that you have good earning ability. You may or may not be careless in your expenditures at times, and you would do well to develop conservatism. It is apparent that you will realize some good returns in investments during your lifetime. It is advisable that you refrain from unwise gambling and speculation. Since you appreciate the good things in life it is natural that you spend much more money thereon. Your general financial outlook is good.

"Although your sign is a fixed one, there is travel in your life, both for business and pleasure. There may or may not be many extensive journeys but it is clearly indicated that you experience at times an urge for traveling to far-off places of the world.

"The indications for social life and friendships are favorable. Your personality will draw friends and acquaintances from all walks of life. You are loyal to your friends and capable of commanding the respect of everyone. At times, an active social life is to your liking; however, there are occasions when you wish solitude, enjoying your thoughts in profound meditation.

"You will find it to your advantage to bring out the constructive qualities of your mind. Do not permit your sensitiveness and obstinacy to rule you. These qualities were given you for a constructive purpose, the sensitiveness to increase your power of perception and perspective while obstinacy, if properly applied and intelligently controlled is conductive to the type of determination which will enable you to appreciate the fruits of success and accomplishment in your efforts. Be careful to exercise good judgment in matters pertaining to love and marriage because of your sensitive nature. Your greatest impulsiveness appears to be emotional rather than mental and herein your difficulty lies. This proves that one of your most beautiful qualities should be carefully and intelligently controlled or it will result in being your worst enemy temporarily. It casts your heart and mental faculties into depths of mental and emotional despair when disillusionment comes. Use good judgment in this regard and you will avoid these heartaches in love.

"Your success in life comes principally as the result of your thinking and capability in applying your efforts in the right direction. You may not show originality in thinking as do people of some of the other signs, but you have the ability to carry on or improve what the originator started. You have more or less to work out your own destiny as you possess an independent nature. You succeed principally by your patience, thoughtfulness and unceasing efforts to overcome obstacles and drive your way to success. You have determination, fortitude, and aggressiveness necessary to progress. You have good mental qualities and are capable of rising above the sphere of your birth in the course of life. You will be benefited by the study of good books and works along the lines of your endeavor or activity."

If it were available, a print of Valentino's hand would be of interest to those familiar with palmistry. Many famous actors and actresses of Hollywood, who have had readings, have left hand prints with palmists, where they have been on exhibition; but I find no record of any of Valentino's hand.

CHAPTER XIV

During the life of any screen star he or she receives "fan" letters in varying numbers. Valentino received what probably aggregated tons of mail.

The letters that come to me concerning Valentino, his crypt, his life and so on; letters containing poems, orders for flowers to be placed close to Rudy's resting place, letters asking innumerable questions and requesting souvenirs, letters that reveal touching human sidelights – they come from young and old, men and women, and from all over the world. Some come at regular intervals, the writers carrying on what amounts to a permanent correspondence.

Some of these correspondents are among the many who have visited the Valentino crypt and with whom I have become personally acquainted – and some of these acquaintanceships have grown into warm friendships. Others are men and women scattered all over the face of the earth who have never been in Hollywood.

One of these is M.C. Elliot, 4 Suffolk Square, Cheltenham, England, who is secretary of the Valentino Association in London. Miss Elliot furnishes the following description of the work which is being done in the name of the actor.

This, we can be sure, is a memorial after Valentino's own heart.

THE VALENTINO ASSOCIATION

"The above movement was inaugurated in London on August 23rd, 1927, in response to many requests from those who were anxious to honour and perpetuate the memory of the great star in a worthy and dignified manner, on lines of which we feel he would have approved. Not as the "Matinee Idol," an angle he disliked, but as the artist who gladly made considerable personal sacrifices to maintain his ideals and to improve screen conditions, and who, by the charm and sincerity of his characterizations, has won for himself an ever living place in the esteem and affection of thousands of every nationality.

Remembering Valentino's generosity to those in need, and his affection for children, the Association concentrates mainly on philanthropic work of a practical and constructive nature.

Our memorials include:---

The Valentino Roof-Garden given to the Italian Hospital in London on May 6th, 1928 and since then, maintained and enlarged.

A cheque for 300 to the same hospital, for the reconstruction and entire re-equipment of a ward, which was officially opened on August 23rd, 1930, as the Valentino Ward for Children. Also a large and urgently-needed ultra-ray lamp for sunlight treatment of adults and children.

Each Christmas, the Association's gifts have been distributed to all the patients and staff, and concerts by London artists and other entertainments are organized for them by us during the year.

During the summer, children from the poorest slums of London enjoy a week in the country as "Valentino's Guests," and at Christmas, hampers are dispatched to needy families.

In 1931 we adopted seven boys of the Dulwich Naval Brigade, a social club for working lads between the ages of 13 and 17. The "Valentino Cadets" are chosen each year from among those with the best all-round records during the preceding twelve months. Twice a year we give a Tea and Entertainment to the whole of the Brigade.

In 1934, we presented 50 special down pillows to St George's Hospital (one of those visited by Valentino when he was in London), and re-equipped the Children's Ward. Concerts are arranged at Christmas.

In addition to sending bundles of clothing, etc., to various refuge-homes and other charitable institutions, in memory of the time when Valentino was friendless and starving, the Association particularly interests itself in the Embankment Fellowship Centre, 59a, Belvedere Road, S.E. 1 (London). This movement is unique in many ways and supplies invaluable and discriminating help to hundreds of those destitute and deserving cases who do not benefit under the new regulations.

The Valentino Association of which the headquarters are in London, is a British organization with an international membership, and has no connection with any other movement in England or abroad. It is non-sectarian and non-political and has no paid officials.

Yearly subscriptions (Members 5/-, Associates 2/6), go towards the costs of printing, postage, etc., all other and personal expenses being defrayed by the officials and members themselves. Thus, donations to any of our Funds are given to these without any deductions.

Further details of the Valentino Association can be had on application to the Honorary Secretary, also books dealing with the life and career of Valentino including his poems, "Day-Dreams."

Adeline Linnel, of 1283 Early Avenue, Chicago, Illinois, is treasurer of Chicago Valentino Memorial Club. The motto of this organization is: "We Do Not Forget." Miss Linnell furnishes the following interesting account.

"During five months at the CENTURY OF PROGRESS EXPOSITION, literally thousands of people paid an extra admission to the "Italian Village" for the express purpose of visiting the "Valentino Exhibit" – which was sponsored by the "Chicago Valentino Memorial Club." The only pure memorial gesture on the grounds, it proved to be one of the outstanding attractions of the Village, and of the Fair.

"Celebrities from all parts of the world lingered long to tell of incidents and to express their undying love and admiration for Rudy; members of the Press, who had interviewed him, many personal friends who knew him intimately, and those who were associated with him in his work – Directors, Technicians, Dancers, one of his Chauffeurs, and servants from his home "Falcon Lair" – all told of his kindness and consideration and many interesting incidents.

"There remains no doubt of the Universal love still cherished for him, as demonstrated by the overwhelming tributes of all races who flocked from other Village concessions, to tell using their own way, that he also belonged to them. (Some, who could not talk with us, gesticulated wildly, to impress us with their sincerity.)

"Valentino's greatest contribution is the world-wide bond of friendship he created. He once remarked that he "*sensed* the kinship of *all* races in his blood.""

"Among the many professional and illustrious personages who placed their autographs in our 'Red Register' came a prominent Judge from the east, who later sent us a copy of his Eulogy, which was broadcast immediately after Rudy's passing.

"Our booth contained the many belongings Rudy had worn and used in his immortal pictures, and was constantly surrounded by eager crowds of people from all corners of the earth; it was a joy to afford them this privilege, and our reward was the pleasure of meeting them and of feeling that our memorial work was not in vain."

There is one in particular who is worthy of mention. While comparisons are difficult and inaccurate, I have called her "Valentino's greatest admirer." In front of me at this moment I have a stack of letters received from her during the past two years, as well as innumerable postcards – all from Miss Emma Leutgeb, Salzburg, Austria. I first heard from her a short time after my story was published in New Movie Magazine. She had read it and then wrote to me. She asked many questions concerning Valentino, his crypt, his brother Alberto, his sister and Mr. Ullman, his business manager. She asked for pictures of his former home on Whitley Heights in Hollywood, of Falcon Lair and the crypt. I obtained all that she asked for, and sent them to her. Her sincerity as expressed in her letter was appealing.

This was followed by the receipt of money from her for flowers to be placed at the crypt on the anniversary of Rudy's death. In her home in Salzburg she has a room dedicated to the memory of Valentino, where her large collection of pictures and souvenirs is kept. Many of these she has placed under glass. Photographs of her Valentino collection have been reproduced in European magazines.

Then, came a letter from Miss Leutgeb asking for authentic information about Rudy's crypt. Was he in his own crypt or were his remains to be buried in the Potter's field? A story had been falsely circulated that Valentino was to be buried near the edge of Potter's field, alone and forgotten; that his brother, Alberto, and sister, would not claim the body. I made haste to answer this letter and state the true facts, sending a picture of the crypt at the same time. This crypt has been purchased by the estate from Mr. Balboni, husband of June Mathis. I had taken this picture at the eighth anniversary of Rudy's death and showed the roses which I had placed before the crypt. I reproduce here the first letter I received form Miss Leutgeb.

Salzburg, 8, March 1933

Dear Sir:
I beg your pardon when I as quite unknown dare addressing from faraway a great request

to you. I was reading of you from New Movie (April 1932) how amiable and kind you are with the visitors who come to see Valentino's tomb.

Having misfortunately no occasion to lay a flower on his tomb, or personally address my request to you, I take the liberty to express my wish by letter.

As I cannot get another souvenir, it is my (wish of my heart) to possess at least anything of his sepulcher, and therefore beg you to send me *a rose of his tomb*. I should be *very happy* to possess such a treasure and would be very much oblige to such an amiability.

That you might know from what country in Europa this letters is coming, I send you a picture cards and accompany the letter with the liveliest wishes, that it may reach your address.

Once more I beg your parden for troubling you with my request, and sign

Yours truly,
Emma Leutgeb.
Please put the flower in a little box so that I get it in good order.
Emma Leutgeb.

Accompanying one letter was a clipping from a Vienna film magazine, which had been illustrated with the picture I had sent. She had induced the magazine to publish the article, "So that every reader of this paper will know that Valentino has a sepulcher of his own, not in a cellar, but in a place where there are floral greetings placed by loving hands."

In all my correspondence with this lady there has been not a word of the "fan" letter atmosphere, simply the profound worship of the memory of Valentino. And this is just one case in many. I value the friendship of the distant Miss Leutgeb very highly.

In another case, I received the following letter from Miss Fanny Lichtenfeld, residing in an Eastern city. It will be noted that Miss Lichtenfeld refers to herself as a Valentino "fan," yet in the course of our correspondence, there has been nothing but reverence for the spirit of the departed Rudy, reverence of a deeply spiritual nature. Valentino has almost been sainted by so many of these correspondents. This first of a long series of letters follows:

Richmond, Va.,
July 18, 1932

Dear Mr. Peterson:
I have read in "The New Movie" magazine how very kind and sympathetic you are in regard to inquiries concerning the late Mr. Rudolph Valentino, so I am taking the liberty of writing to you in the hope that you may be able to help me. I am sending this letter to you under registered cover, so there will be less probability of its becoming lost in the mail.

Like thousands of Mr. Valentino's fans, his sainted memory is fresh in my heart, and I am very anxious to send to his crypt a floral remembrance on the anniversary of his passing on. Do you think I could get a pretty one for five or six dollars, and with what florist in Hollywood, or through whom should I place my order? Perhaps if I would not be putting you to too much trouble, you could handle this direct for me? I would send you money order in the above amount, or, if there be a delivery charge, I would be glad to send the additional sum.

As it takes about six days for a letter to reach Hollywood from Richmond, Va., wont you kindly write me (stating whether the above amount would be adequate) in time for you to receive my reply by August 23? I would make the remittance on August 15. Enclosed please find stamped addressed envelope for your convenience.

With best wishes for your health, and hoping you will be able to help me, for which I would be grateful to you *always*, I am

Sincerely yours,
Fanny Lichtenfeld.

As in the case of Miss Leutgeb, through correspondence Miss Lichtenfeld has become a valued friend.

Many poems are received. Some of these are of high quality. One which has been published, written by Irene Cole MacArthur, follows:

To RUDOLPH VALENTINO

So he is dead, who gave his magic art
To lift from dreary ruts our humdrum world;
Whose skillful touch could reach into the heart
And leave its strings with lovely notes impearled
That haunted even dreams, harmonious
With all that love means in reality.
They blasphemed, they who called him "screen sheik," thus
Thinking to pay him honor, thoughtlessly
Acclaiming the perfect rose a common weed.
Could they his Julio so soon forget?
Do Beaucaire's wistful lips still vainly plead
"A man is just a name"? Banish regret –
Because so much of beauty, grace and power
Could go before, ah surely we shall be
More unafraid of that dividing hour
Between time's death and life's eternity.
Call him the perfect lover, not in scorn,
For love itself is perfect, but remembering
That since this sad old world was born
That God himself has given no sweeter thing
To man than love, for He Himself is love.
Though he seems dead, he who so freely gave
So much of beauty to drab lives, above
Somewhere out from this early grave,
His spirit shall go winging through the years
Triumphant to the Master Loving-Heart.
And men shall try to copy through vain tears
The matchless, living beauty of his art.

Mary Burke Rich, of Hollywood, has a collection of Valentino pictures, clippings from magazines and newspapers and scrapbooks. She has written frequent tributes to Rudy, one of which follows:

VALENTINO TALKS WITH LIFE

"Glad to welcome you, Life." Thus spoke the Great Lover, Valentino. "How is that world out there that used to be mine? Life—it seems to me they are killing Love out there! Don't they know that I am the master of Love? I taught them to respect and love Love; that it is all in life. And now, they have almost murdered him. Life, I have a message for them, from my palace Regent: I am not dead! I am still living still, and at some time I shall call them before my throne, and they shall answer for murder."

"And, Master Valentino," said Life, "that is why I kneel before your throne tonight. I have message – I have sorrow—I have trouble, and I bring you thousands of dead loves to revive. You have hundreds where'er you dwell. Beyond your door in the graveyard yonder, you have countless more. But the saddest of them all, Master are the dying loves beyond the gates. Poor souls wrestling with life's storm beaten mystery of life. They are but flotsam and jetsam dashed by angry waves. My Master, it is this I come to ask you: Will you call by bugle and with trumpet loud and make them kneel before your throne? Tell them, Master! LOVE IS ALL OF LIFE AND MORE."

"Honor to you, Life, for the message you bear. Long have I meditated in my tomb, where the days and nights are but one – and I have heard the dying cries from great loves beyond – and the shoveling of the earth that closed out their woes forever. I could no longer stand those cries. Life, my crypt opened. It's door fell beneath my feet. I stood in the palace. I swept through the corridor doors, and through the great gates I passed – Life, I am with you again," he said, as he took his arm and meditatively walked out into the great world. "Life!" said Valentino, "Let us teach them what they could not learn in life."

While the letter that follows is, perhaps, a little long for publication here, it is interesting for one reason inasmuch as it is one of the hundreds telling of various Valentino Associations, Clubs, etc. The writer of this letter – and it is only one from the same individual – has sent souvenirs from Barbados and is constantly interested in the memory of Valentino. Here is the letter:

Belleville
Barbados, W.L.
Oct. 20th, 1932

Dear Mr. Peterson:
I received your letter three days ago and thank you very much for sending me the very nice postcard in colors showing one of the elegant corridors at the H. Cemetery. It is beautiful to

see how it is kept and all the bright and pretty flowers arranged so nicely in their spaces. It makes such a pretty scene. Thanks for your letter and for the explanation on the postcard. I can imagine about where Valentino's resting place is by your description. The scene that is depicted in the window, does that represent the scene beyond the window outside? And what is the little square to the side (like a picture) in the window? And is there another corridor beyond the post in the middle of the window part?

I obtained two copies of the April New Movie Magazine and read your article with *great* interest indeed. I sent at once for one copy from the Tower Magazines, Inc., N. Jersey, Publishers, and in writing a lady friend in New York, she was lucky in getting one, and sent it to me, too. I since let a lady friend here have one, who was very interested also in reading it. I think your article is *exceedingly interesting* and it is certainly wonderful that so much as taken place and is still taking place at his crypt. He was indeed beloved. I saw all you said, too, about June Mathis Balboni, and how it was through her that he rose to the fame he did, and all also explained about her in your article in the magazine. I see his crypt is in the S.E. part of the mausoleum, and the flowers are kept so nice and fresh by Mrs. Coppola. She is indeed very faithful, and even her little one had been called after him, which is unique.

I am wondering what was done at this sixth anniversary of his death; no doubt quite a lot, as in former years, if not more. The chapel must be perfectly beautiful. If you ever have an interior view of this on a postcard I shall be pleased to have it also. There are indeed a wonderful number of crypts in the large mausoleum, and many more besides that. The illustrations in the magazine are beautiful of the mausoleum, and statue erected in his honour, and the ones of Rudy are so splendid, I think, and so good of him. I notice also the one of yourself, and it is very interesting to me to have such an interesting and fascinating account, which I like to take up and read over and over. It seems *perfectly tragic* that he was "*gone*" at such an early age. I think I told you I have the story of his life written by S. George Ullman, and also his poetry, called "Day Dreams," and many pictures taken at various times that I had come across.

I had read in your article of the basket of flowers being delivered every Saturday as an order from somewhere in England, and here you mention it as the "Valentino Association," which arranges this. It is a very fine and beautiful idea. I had heard of this Association, and the little paper you had before wrapped the 2 beaded flowers in had the address of the secretary, a Miss Elliot, so I immediately wrote her for the particulars of same, etc., and I have had a most interesting reply since from her and all the Association does, and how it is connected with a Station Hospital for children; also the programme of what they were doing from Aug. 21st and on Aug. 23rd for the patients and staff, being the anniversary time. They also take in grown-up people in the Hospital, and not only for children. The particulars she sent me are very interesting, and all about what the Association is doing. Her address is Miss M.G. Elliot, 4 Suffolk Square, Cheltenham, Glos., England.

The Association was formed in London, England in 1927 in response from many requests from those who were anxious to honour and perpetuate his memory, and the circular she sent me explains all about the idea and all the interests concerned and what the subscriptions are, and also mentions the Hollywood Memorial. I shall be replying to her shortly and mention your interesting article.

I enclose a little map and guide of Barbados on which are some views of the Island. I thought this was more interesting than the little souvenir book, as it shows and tells much more. You will note the explanation of the pictures, and all the information on the other side about the Island.

What does the statue represent on the round stone ball in the park erected to Rudy's honor? And what do all the words say at bottom of it? And I see they want to erect a new memorial.

I take the "Film Pictorial" little magazine. The one for Sept. 3rd has an interesting piece about him and a picture, and mentions Miss Elliot and the Association. It is very interesting and is published at Tallis House, Tallis Street, London E.C. 4, England.

Hoping for your reply and with kind wishes.

Sincerely

E. Eckel.

It is unnecessary to reprint more of the stacks of letters that I have at hand. I have chosen only a few at random in order to give an idea of this world-wide, sustained interest. In closing, however, I add two poems. The first embossed in gift and framed for distribution, was placed at the crypt by its author.

A MEMORIAL WITH CHRISTMAS MIRTH
For
RUDOLPH VALENENTINO

He is risen, so they say,
From earth to heaven he is gone.
The Herald Angel did not delay
Providing a robe and a crown
When once he found that the time had come.
His immortal from earth to heaven was born
To the dawn of eternal day.
He is risen, not sad to know,
The conquering power he hath won.
Undoubtedly love on us he bestows,
For heaven gives plays for hits own.
His dwelling is not in this tomb of clay;
He is gone to heaven, not to hell I did say,
For I know the victory he won.

If we could peek through a window of His
That mansion of fame up there,
Of Chrysolite, jasper, and Sardonix,
There would be wonders of mirth we could share.

For heaven is not old, it is always new,
And Christmas most wonderful true.
For Christ Himself is Host of that feast
That we know is well-spread for you,

For loving Rudolph, you.
Composed by Miss Emma Klevberg

The second poem was left with flowers at the crypt on the eleventh anniversary of Valentino's death.

RUDOLPH VALENTINO

Shine on bright star of love, romance and hope.
Let not thy light be dinned by lesser stars,
Whose steady flame burns brightly on
And will not be denied their fate.

Lead thou the way to brighter rays of light,
Where burns the lamp of destiny, eternal.
Shine down on us who've watched your glory fade,
Yet hath not died, and never shall.

L.E.B.

Mrs. Mary E. Palmer, a loyal and ardent admirer of Valentino, makes monthly visits to his tomb, bringing fresh flowers from her garden. As an expression of her love and affection for him, she composed the following.

A TRIBUTE
FROM THE MOTHERS OF THE WORLD
TO
Rudolph Valentino
(Rudolph Guglielmi)

Born in Castelleneta, Italy, May 6th, 1895, 3 A.M.
Went to sleep New York City, August 23rd, 1926. 12:10 P.M

"He marched steadily on until he became one of the most amazing figures of our time."

Set sail for America, Dec. 9th, 1913
Landing in New York, Dec. 23rd, 1913

Noted Dramas: --
"Four Horsemen""Sheik"
"Blood and Sand"   "Son of a Sheik"

RUDOLPH VALENTINO
AS A MOTHER SAW HIM

"In one of his interviews, Valentino remarked that he received more mail from women of mature years than from the younger class. No doubt in song and story all classes of society have written of and about him, of whom has been said: -- *'He marched steadily on until he became one of the most amazing figures of our time?'* But, we have seen no word penned from the mothers, for whom he had such reverence. In honor of them who have so faithfully loved and admired him, we write these lines; in memory of R.V.

"In the days when the world was young and the gods were kind, men looked to them to birth a genius; when maturity of thought came on the plane of vital living, we were taught to look to our grandmothers for the faith that would bring results. Paul says in Timothy: -- 'When I call to remembrance, the unfinished faith that is in thee, which dwelt first in thy grandmother, Lois, and thy mother, Eunice, and, I am persuaded in thee also. Therefore I put thee in remembrance, that thou stir up the gift of God, *that which is in thee.'*

"So, we have the first Bishop to the Gentile world, strong in spiritual and mental ability; the product first of his grandmother, *Lois.*"

"In Algeria, North Africa, beautiful for situation, as to landscape, sky and water; where the mingling of ancestral blood perpetuating the families of beautiful types, so often seen in the North Barbary State --. The gorgeous sunsets and afterglow of the blue and golden sky melting into a royal purple all studded with silver stars, lent enchantment to the Plaza and Moorish balconies. The glowing colors of shawls and scarf's so gracefully worn with the lace mantles on heads and shoulders of Senoritas, Dons, Donnas, Duennas; gave grace and charm to the mighty scenes, as they promenaded on the Plaza or sat on the balconies, listening to the stirring strains of the French Military Band, giving its every evening concert. It was stationed there, with the Royal Regiment in the North African capital, to protect the French interests against the restlessness of the Arabs and their many tribes, who were galling under the yoke of heavy taxes which they felt was an unjust burden and a disgrace to their ancient tribal ancestry of Benjamin and the promise of the land to them through their long line of Abrahamic origin.

"All the homes, with true oriental hospitality, were thrown open to entertainment of officers of rank and authority as well as to the general soldiery.

"To the many noted fetes attended by the ranking officers, in all their brilliant uniforms and flashing accoutrements, many hearts were won to them.

"Among the dark-eyed Senoritas attending this special fete was little La Reta Donato, with eyes and grace of the gazelle, the much beloved and orphan daughter of stately old Don Juan Donato, 'who for the first time in her 16 years had been permitted to attend one of these gay assemblies with her father and Duenna.' How the girlish heart was thrilled with wonder, in this fairyland of animated coloring and music.

"In attendance also, was an Army Surgeon, noted for his skill in plastic surgery; who soon had glances for no one but beautiful, tender-eyed La Reta Donato. His fame and position gave him entrée to the most noted and reserved homes. His entrance into the parental castle of the Senor Donato soon flowered into nuptial rites. Shortly after this mutual union he, with his young wife, were withdrawn to France on furlough.

"The outcome of this happy union was a girl in whose eyes always lingered tender wistfulness. They called her Gabriella in memory of their first tender love glances that drew them to each other in that memorable fete in the gay North African capital.

"Born in France and there educated among stirring scenes of revolution and siege, strengthened in her all the romantic traits of her mother's native climate incorporated with Church training; giving her a devotional realization of God combined with all the courtly chivalry of her French father.

"In the combination of these ideals was birthed an imagination beautiful in coloring and rich in harmonious blending of all qualities that give perfect character of the world.

In years, equally as tender as her mother's, she was united in the bonds that man cannot sever to Captain Giovani Guglielmi, an Italian Cavalry officer. It seems to have been a union of perfect ideals that we glimpse now and then on life's highway. Always to such unions comes one that is the embodiment of perfectly united thought. This baby, in its mother's arms, she looks upon and realizes –

"That it is now apart,
But was once within,
Builded securely, away from sin,
Fashioned together by love untold
A house of ivory, all covered with gold!
' ---- That only a mother's eye can see
As she holds this breath of Eternity.
And nothing about it can make her sad
For, she looks on her travail of Soul, and is glad!'

"So, Rudolph Valentino was born at the appointed time, the genius of the household, who often tired of play and watching his father care for his work, as a veterinary surgeon, through which a love of horses was early developed in him. He would come to his little mother and ask for a story. She was never too busy to turn from her pleasant duties and answer the questionings of the wistful appeal in his eyes; for she well knew what it meant to a growing childish mind to give helpful knowledge when they desired it.

"Cuddled in her arms, she would take from the loom of memory the many weavings of her childhood days, and in that garment of such vital history, enfolded, he would live with her again, in castle halls of his grandsire of ancient splendor and regal glory. And then with her life through the siege of Paris that was soul-stirring and breath-taking, he would look and listen, entranced, until he would see her in a halo of rapture, and she became his sainted ideal of womanhood. . . and with that halo of tender expression he never ceased to crown and reverence woman. It was like finding the "last carol" in the hearts of the women of all the world, that carved for him a niche that he would forever fill.

"We are told that 'the mills of the gods grind slowly, but they grind exceeding fine.' When the world was heart-torn and bleeding between the upper and nether mill-stone of man's selfishness, in making a war, shedding the blood of millions of innocent souls and wrecking human trust and brotherhood the world over. That human unnaturalness in its insane scramble for another man's country; regarding no man's right to life, liberty, and honorable ownership, this time Divine Providence, from the sunrise of the old creative world, to the youthful glow of the new, in its onward Western march of invention and reckless hurry, brought – Rodolpho Guglielmi (who became Our Rudy.) Glowing with the naturalness of human self-expression to give to the great congregations of the Churches of the world (the theatres) the portrayal of a love, so healing, helpful and sustaining in its whole-heartedness . . . that it was like a divine breath sent to cool the parched and fevered brow of a war-sickened world and blood-soaked earth. In the midst of it all he felt keenly the loneliness of it all. Far from sunny Italy and those of kindred ties and speech, he was gong through the state of being that 'God abhors as nature does'; the vacuum of loneliness – to offset the creeping in of this baleful spectre, God, creates in perfection of pairs; male, female – that 'As the bow is to the arrow; useless one without the other –.' He desired companionship and mutual understanding. But never at the expense of modesty and true chivalry. He sought, but it was illusive, 'a ship that passed in the night.' With chaste dignity he rescued this delicate situation from the contumacy of public opinion; without the least shade of rudeness. For his one desire was love, without reproach or regret. . .

"In that darkest hour of human need, all alone, alone in the silent chamber of sorrow, he wrestled, as Jacob of old, and would not cease until deliverance came.

"Then, as the sun of hope arose on the new day, a love was birthed! A love divine! All love excelling! The love of heaven to earth come down! Now, anointed with a smile, so rare and fleeting; masculine and feminine entwined, neither losing the strength of the other; almost defying the artist's skill to confine it to the camera – he smiled – when, *he knew*, that when all else failed, this altruistic, vicarious love would *abide*!

"And, that, which encircled the strength of his forearm, the bracelet; heretofore the emblem of an untiring devotion became the symbol of a crushed and withered ideal. Willingly he made it a cross, by which he suffered reproach, that *he* might become impersonal to each individual in building their own concept of altruistic, sacrificial love from the realities of his different portrayals of human character, without a visible hindrance.

"The knowledge of this indwelling love was the strength of his genius. Now, nothing else mattered. Only a passionate desire remained. . . . that his creative world might be made happy, and he, like the Savior of men might be *understood*.

"With this cord of selfless giving in our hands we draw the curtain apart on the living drama of his heart-hold on the world. From now on the magic wand of true creative idealism in its most perfect form is seen.

'The Four Horsemen of the Apocalypse.'

"When called the most unselfish man in the regiment because he was fighting and giving his life for another man's country and transgression.

"She, in the home with the war blind husband, (of cruel made family law) recognizing the travesty of it all, and feeling the burden of separation more than her heart could endure. Tempted to flee! Unselfish love . . . from that dreadful nightmare of mud and misery! The battle front! Keeping watch at night in a drenching, chilling rain, with his one true friend! A friend that was sticking closer than a blood relative. The little Argentine monkey. Together they looked upon the face of *her*, and the unselfishness of vicarious love, on battle front and home, birthed in *her* a new sense of creative devotion. And the vision gave her strength and courage, to go on and glorify her vow. . . As soothing as a breath of spikenard, freshened by dew, and blown o'er by the south wind, rich with its fragrance . . . Is the scene in the Casa de Campo, when he quickly stepped before the bridal door of the cama domier of his wife, and would not allow the woman, who sought to betray him, to enter. To him, marriage was a holy Sacrament. The nuptial chamber, the pledged place of his one and only love . . . a sacred shrine that hallowed the way to motherhood!

"The nobleness of the gesture was in his quick, unconscious portrayal of his innate character; protecting all that was divinely sacred to him. The ever to be remembered scene in 'Blood and Sand.'"

The Sheik

"That masterpiece of character building, of the soul's awakening, and the undying devotion to pure womanhood, will ever stand a monument in the Hall of Immortals; with him, Shakespeare, who learned at his mother's knee (Mary Arden) the mystery of the Bible, and wove it, in later years, into the poetry of dramatics, through his love of Anne Hathaway. And she, who, in the days of '70, when her Nation stood in grave peril, through the heroism of her blood, stirred it to patriotism and victory. . . Sarah Bernhardt.

"The one thing dear to the heart of an Arab dweller on the desert, whether to tribe or household *his word* governs! In this day, when parental authority is so lightly regarded, it is refreshing to see how he submits to his Arab father's command, through it suffering great humiliation to his youthful manhood, yet, obeys. Surely this giving in of his strong inherited will comes like a benediction to the home in the making. Then, with approval of parents to the union, like a knight-errant of the days of chivalry and great loves, on the steed of perfect control, breaking through the forests of ignorance and malicious superstition, to the castle of Divine Love. . . that she within might be awakened, as was the Sleeping Beauty, to the realization and sacredness of creative force.

"This, thoroughly seen and accented by 'teen folks, would forever settle the question of birth control and breaking of marriage vows; and give the judges over the divorce courts a great deal of time to take naps.

"Happy the woman, even on the screen, who could mother such nobility.

"Happy the youths who could profit by such manly dignity.

"Happy the soil that could call him son!

"Happy the Land, who his adoption won!

Requiescence!
(Rest – Repose)

"As the twilight deepens, and the shadows lengthen, and night, wonderful night, mysterious night, coming on, with its fire-flies, and its paradise of starts . . . and sleepy time! What better pillow to rest his head upon than the 'Sheik'? All feathered with promises, 'He that dwelleth in the secret place (love) of the most High, He shall cover with his feathers.'

"And the coverlet, the 'Son of the Sheik' with its riot of Oriental colors, so symphonically blended and knitted together, in a way as fascinating and alluring as the evening stories of Scheherazade, that charmed and wooed sleep to the Sultan for a 'thousand nights.' And with the loving touch of a loving mother's hand, it is tucked around his manly boyish self, as he snuggles down and whispers with tired voice . . . *Ma mere* . . . *Ma petite mere* . . . To rest, to awaken! To come with the sunlight he loved so well . . . For he will come!

On God's golden morn
And Live on this earth, made new.
In the light of that sunshine
He loved so well –
Will have all of his dreams
Come true!

"Happy, thrice happy, indeed should we be. As a treasure house now, we hold all of his hopes, all of live.

'Till the Sands of the Desert grow cold.'"
Mrs. Mary E. Palmer
Pasadena, California

95

Valentino Remembered

Floral tributes abound for the 4th anniversary of his death, August 23, 1930

Unidentified Lady In Black places her floral offering on August 23, 1937

Aunt Teresa Werner, (with arm on ledge at crypt) was willed one third of
Valentino's estate is joined by friends and fans on August 23, 1938

Yet another unidentified Lady In
Black, circa 1938

Various fans converge at the crypt to remember Rudolph Valentino, circa August 23, 1939

Placing flowers for her
Rudy, circa 1938

Lady In Black Ditra
Flame bows her head in
remembrance at the crypt
of Rudolph Valentino,
August 23, 1941

Unnamed
youngsters dressed
in Sheik costumes,
place their flowers
at the crypt in this
undated photograph

Rudolph Valentino's brother Alberto Valentino, left, thanks Belle Martell and another
Valentino Memorial participant, in front of his brother's resting place. Circa late 1950's

John Wayne Caley, 18, right, and Josee Metricks, 17, left, dressed in Gaucho costumes for the 25th anniversary of the Valentino Memorial Service on August 23, 1951

June Wood, left, and James Kirkwood, right, place floral tributes to Valentino on August 23, 1961

Michael Back, left, and Mary Pfalzgraff, right, in front of Valentino's crypt. Michael holds an oversized framed photo of Rudy and one of Valentino's personal walking canes.

AFTERWORD

Just how Roger C. Peterson obtained the position as custodian of the Cathedral Mausoleum at the Hollywood Memorial Park Cemetery in 1927 was a clouded mystery. Now, with recent access to the legendary Lady In Black Ditra Flame's private correspondence, its found that it is quite possible that she played a hand in this.

Roger Peterson was born on May 20, 1903 in Duluth, Minnesota, his father Charles F. Peterson and his mother Betsy Johnson were both natives of Sweden. As a working youth and into adulthood, Peterson held a bevy of various jobs including working in a tire factory, in an assembly plant, saw mills, paper mills and even on a railroad construction crew. He also worked in the Dakota harvesting season, but it was his deep passion for writing that drew him to California.

This is where Ditra Flame steps into the story. She retained copies of all letters sent to her, as well as letters that she sent out. In an undated letter to Roger Peterson, Ditra reminds Peterson how they first met saying "I had my music studio on Coronado Street, you came to my door looking for someone who's address you couldn't find….you asked to use my telephone -- you came into my studio after you phoned - we talked - you said you wanted to be writer - I told you I was writing in my spare time - you said you wanted to write an article about Valentino - I showed you my Rudolph Valentino scrap book - remember? - You said you'd like to interview people at Rudy's tomb but didn't know how - I told you that was easy - just get a job at the mausoleum."

That fateful meeting with Flame made for a unique alliance. Peterson would ultimately go on to successfully obtain the position just as Ditra had suggested. Peterson was the official custodian at the Cemetery Mausoleum where Valentino lied buried - working there from 1927 until 1940.

With his new position within the mausoleum under way, he began to keep a diary of the endless flood of people who daily sought out Valentino's resting place. Many confided to Peterson that Rudy had appeared to them in a vision or dream, compelling them to visit his tomb. Many of the stories were touching and heartbreaking. Peterson himself felt at a loss as how to explain what he was witnessing. He wanted to make certain the reader understood that he wasn't embellishing, saying "there is neither exaggeration nor a striving for effect in what I give here. I am setting down facts as I know them, in order that the problem which puzzles me may be made clear to others. There must be a reason for these things." Peterson went on to rhetorically ask "why is his resting place visited every day of the year by this continuous procession of men and women from near and far? There must be some cause deeper than idle curiosity or mere hero worship. In that fact lies the mystery."

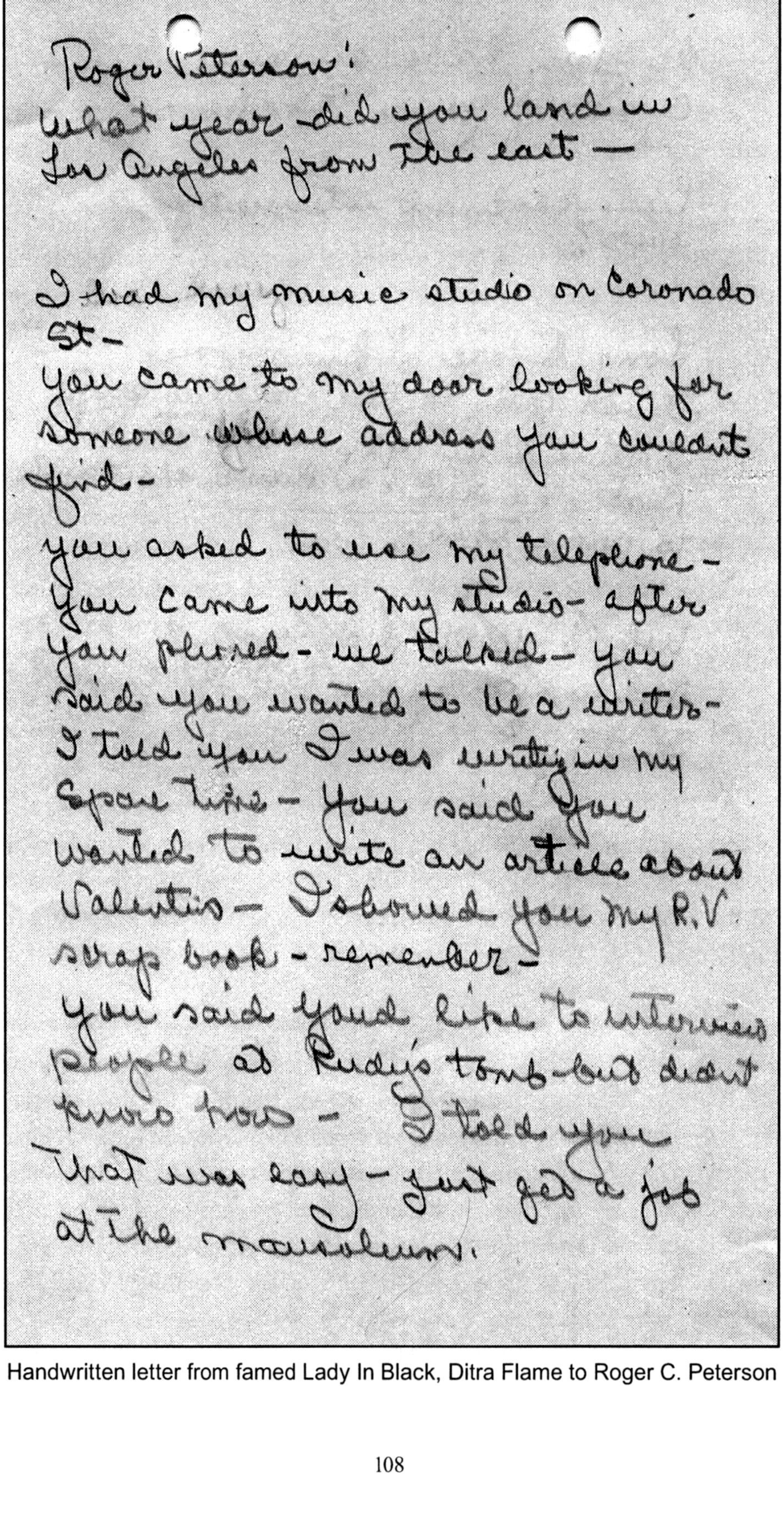

Roger Peterson:
what year did you land in
Los Angeles from the east —

I had my music studio on Coronado
St —
You came to my door looking for
someone whose address you couldn't
find —
You asked to use my telephone —
You came into my studio — after
you phoned — we talked — You
said you wanted to be a writer —
I told you I was writing in my
spare time — You said you
wanted to write an article about
Valentino — I showed you my R.V.
scrap book — remember —
You said you'd like to interview
people at Rudy's tomb — but didn't
know how — I told you
that was easy — just get a job
at the mausoleum.

Handwritten letter from famed Lady In Black, Ditra Flame to Roger C. Peterson

108

Valentino fan Leon Massey, left, poses with Roger Peterson
on the front steps of the Cathedral Mausoleum, circa 1937

My Strange Experiences
at VALENTINO'S GRAVE

Roger Peterson's first foray into publishing came with the April 1932 edition of *The New Movie Magazine.* Culling incidents from his diary, now with five years worth of entries, Peterson was able to write his first article about Valentino. Titled *My Strange Experiences at Valentino's Grave,* the article promised the reader "the astonishing day-by-day story of the man who has guarded Valentino's tomb for five years." The introduction to the article was written by Jack Grant and set the groundwork for the interesting stories "Pete" would be telling. For this first article selected dates from Peterson's diary were utilized, in a straight forward style. A sample entry reads:

> **August 24, 1928** I don't know what I am going to do with all these flowers. George Ullman, who was Valentino's manager sent over a lot more today. He gets letters and telegrams from all over the world containing remittances for floral tributes. His secretary sees that everyone is represented by some blossoms. This she does with great care, as she holds it a high honor to serve the ones who loved Valentino. She personally selects each floral offering and spends hours helping me arrange them. That is she arranges them and I help if I can. We had our usual group of hysterical women yesterday and today. I am becoming accustomed to women screaming and crying for their "Rudy." But when men do it, it sort of gets me. There was a little foreigner in today, a Frenchman, I think. He burst into tears and kissed the cold marble of Valentino's crypt, then turning, he practically ran from the building.

Not every visitor was as dramatic. One such person Peterson got to know and look forward to seeing each time was Mrs. Coppola. He met her on October 15, 1928 when her baby, who had died at birth, was buried in the top tier in the same corridor that Valentino rested in. She even named her infant Rodolfo, in honor of Rudy. In her grief Mrs. Coppola would come to her babies grave and spend several hours reading her Bible and praying. Over time she and Peterson, whom she called "Mr. Pete," developed a warm friendship. In the following diary entry he wrote of her own Valentino encounter.

> **November 24, 1928** Mrs. Coppola was happier today than I have

ever seen her. I asked her why and she told me a strange story of Valentino coming to her last night and talking to her. She said his spirit came to her house and knocked on the door. When she let him in, he told her that her baby was happy and not to grieve so much.

The grave of baby Rodolfo Coppola in the top tier of the Valentino corridor is no longer there. However, in its place there is a marker for Angelina Coppola listed as "Beloved Mother" with her date of death listed as 1956. Perhaps when she was laid to rest, her infant son Rodolfo was reunited with his mother. The cemetery records for this era were hand written and didn't always include the removal or addition to remains.

Peterson continued his job at the Cathedral mausoleum, all the while adding daily entries into his diary. In his spare time he continued his writing. He ventured to a western theme for three fictional stories he penned for *Western Story Magazine*. The first of these appeared in their October 19, 1935 edition entitled *Cowboy's Hunch*. This quickly followed publication in the same month with *Blizzard Fury*. His final story for the magazine came just in time for the new year, published January 4, 1936 called *Fishing Lawman*. These pulp western magazines were sold for fifteen cents an issue and were popular with adults as well as children. *Western Story Magazine* was first published in 1919 and ran forty years until it ceased publication in September 1949.

The year 1936 would mark a decade since Valentino's death and the movie magazines were already creating a buzz among their readers about how well Rudy was remembered. Timed perfectly for the 10th anniversary, *Film Pictorial* magazine in their August 22, 1936 edition printed Roger Peterson's latest Valentino article *Why Valentino Will Never Be Forgotten*.

Peterson proclaimed "the germ of my desire to write the story took life and grew from my amazement at the never ceasing parade of people seeking the Valentino crypt." He went on to tell the reader that the sheer volume of visitors was staggering. "It was not surprising that following the interment in Hollywood, (1926) visitors and mourners were very frequent. But it is reason for surprise that now, ten years after the man's death the number of these has increased rather than diminished."

Western Story magazine published three of Petersons fictional western short stories

It was after the publishing of this article that Peterson would find himself flooded with correspondence. People wrote to Peterson pleading for him to send them a mere pedal from a rose that adorned Valentino's crypt. Many had specific questions, inquiring about the Lady In Black or the rumor that Valentino had been forgotten. Some were inquisitive as to articles pertaining to Valentino that they had read, and were asking for verification if he was to be moved, and if so, when. The original plans for a lavish resting place officially ended when the Valentino estate, administered by Bank of America, purchased the crypt #1205 from Sylvano Balboni on March 24, 1933. The price paid to Balboni was $800.00

This continued frenzy of interest about the day-to-day happenings at the Valentino crypt spurred Roger Peterson to finalize a dream of his. The previous year, he had discretely written to the treasurer of the Chicago Valentino Memorial Club, Mrs. Linnell. In his letter to Mrs. Linnell, dated March 22, 1935, he confided in her that "I have about completed the book of which I told you." He went on to ask Mrs. Linnell if she could give him some probable sales figures that he could present to an "interested" publisher of "the probable sale of the book to your club membership, or to any other groups you know about."

Los Angeles, California
1027 W. Kensington Road
March 22, 1935

Mrs. Linnell,
Treasurer Valentino Memorial Club,
1283 Early Avenue
Chicago, Illinois.

Dear Mrs. Linnell:

     I am sorry that I was unable to send you the wreaths you requested for the Valentino memorial at the Fair. They were too cumbersome to be shipped in any way that would assure their safe arrival. I gave a member of your club a large piece of the beaded wreath, which she said she sent to you.

     I have about completed the book of which I told you. It occurs to me that it might be well to include in it some account of the Valentino memorial, of which you had charge during the Fair. The interest shown, the approximate number of visitors, any striking incidents in connection with it — I shall appreciate anything you can tell me about it.

     And will you please give me, in a form which I may present to an interested publisher, the probable sale of the book to your club membership, or to any other groups you know about?

     Sincerely yours,

        Roger C. Peterson

1935 letter from Roger Peterson to Adeline Linnell. Mrs. Linnell was the treasurer of the Valentino Memorial Club of Chicago

VALENTINO
THE UNFORGOTTEN

BY
ROGER C. PETERSON

AUTHOR OF
WHY VALENTINO WILL NEVER BE FORGOTTEN
—Film Pictorial Magazine (London)

MY STRANGE EXPERIENCES AT VALENTINO'S CRYPT
—New Movie Magazine

ALSO NUMEROUS SHORT STORIES

WETZEL PUBLISHING CO., INC.
LOS ANGELES, CALIFORNIA

Valentino The Unforgotten book front-piece from the original edition

Roger Peterson inscribed a copy of his book on August 5, 1938,
to Miss Alba C. Yanni whom he called
"a very sweet Italian girl who paid a visit to Valentino's tomb."

By this point Peterson was working full speed ahead on the Valentino book project. Taking a variation of his 1936 article's title (*Why Valentino Will Never Be Forgotten*) Peterson reworked the name of his new book to be more simplistic and straight forward. It would be called *Valentino The Unforgotten.*

The Library of Congress registered the copyright on December 24, 1937. Wetzel Publishing Company in Los Angeles California was the publisher for a Spring 1938 release. Along with stories cultivated from his diary of visitors and happenings at the Valentino crypt, Peterson added additional chapters to round out his tome. This would include chapters on various Valentino Associations, and one on a "Graphological analysis of Rudolph Valentino" which analyzed his handwriting, all without telling the expert in advance, who's writing it was.

Chapter ten would prove to be the most puzzling. Entitled *The Mysterious Veiled Lady In Black*, it raised many eyebrows. While Peterson had clearly been an eye-witness to a parade of numerous would-be Ladies In Black over the course of the early years, his decisive exclusion of Ditra Flame from the throng of would-be heirs to the title is highly mystifying.

It's not apparent if some falling out occurred between Flame and Peterson in the ensuing years of their first encounter when he used her telephone, to the time, years later, when he published his book *Valentino The Unforgotten.* In her letter to Peterson, Ditra appeared to harbor no serious ill-will towards Peterson but in her correspondence she gently reprimanded him that "long before I knew you, I was going to the Valentino crypt. I always wore black and a veil. I have affidavits to prove this."

For what ever his reasons, Peterson did not include any mention of Flame in is book. However Ditra needn't worry. Few would ever read of it. The first run printing of *Valentino The Unforgotten* was completed in early 1938 and one small shipment was dispatched to book stores. A fire broke out in the warehouse that evening and the entire remaining inventory went up in smoke. Nothing remained.

With this shocking news, naturally Peterson was devastated. This was his dream literally crushed and going up in smoke. Peterson trudged on in his daily duties as custodian for almost two more years before quietly departing his position. When he left, disillusioned in 1940, there would no longer be a full time custodian on duty within the Cathedral mausoleum, and to date that has never changed. Truly with his departure, it closed the end of an era.

It's some-what sketchy as to what entirely happened to Peterson after he left his position. Documents show that he started a new career, that of being a home contractor, self employed, installing heating and ventilation systems in homes. Roger Peterson successfully maintained this line of work for over twenty years.

Roger Peterson assists an unnamed Lady In Black, by carrying
her floral tribute to the crypt, circa 1938

During this time, he resided with his wife Muriel whom he lovingly pet-named "Sugar" at 748 ½ North Vendome in Silverlake, California. His son Roger B. Peterson lived not far, on Olmstead Drive, in Glendale California.

When multiple health issues, including emphysema, manifested, Roger Peterson entered Glenoaks Convalescent Hospital located at 409 West Glenoaks Blvd in Glendale, CA. It would be here that Roger C. Peterson, the no-nonsense "Mr. Pete," the custodian of Valentino's grave for numerous years, would pass away with his family at his side, on July 31, 1972.

Roger Peterson would be laid to rest two days later, on August 2, 1972, next to his wife at Grand View Memorial Park Cemetery, in Glendale California occupying a dual plot. The services were conducted under the direction of Kiefer and Eyerick Mortuary.

Roger C. Peterson's grave located at Grand View Memorial
Park in Glendale California Section M, Lot 528

Roger C. Peterson was a first hand eye-witness, on a daily basis, to the most ardent of Valentino's fans. He admitted that he had a short fuse for what he deemed as nonsense – even to his hard line attitude of tears from male fans in the early years. He alone documented the comings and goings at the crypt of Rudolph Valentino. He interacted with Alberto Valentino, Jean Acker and scores of others in the never ending sea of humanity visiting the grave of Rudolph Valentino. Roger Peterson's *Valentino The Unforgotten* is also unique in Hollywood history in that never before (or since) has a book been published about visitors to the grave of a Hollywood star.

On August 23, 1937, the 11ᵗʰ anniversary of Valentino's death had just been observed. Although Peterson's entry in his diary that day reflected his thoughts pertaining to that particular year, his foresight to the future proved to be very keen.

The eleventh anniversary of Valentino's death has passed. Others will follow, but if they reveal a fraction of the loyalty and devotion which marked this one, in numbers of visitors and in gorgeous display of floral offerings to Rudy's memory, I will know that the man will never be forgotten.

Roger C. Peterson
August 23, 1937

CPSIA information can be obtained at www.ICGtesting.com
Printed in the USA
LVOW032211120812

294034LV00001B/54/A

9 781425 996734